PERFECT
PERENNIALS
for the Prairie Gardener

PERFECT PERENNIALS

for the Prairie Gardener

Dawn Vaessen

FIFTH
HOUSE

Published by
Fifth House Ltd.
A Fitzhenry & Whiteside Company
195 Allstate Parkway
Markham, ON L3R 4T8
www.fifthhousepublishers.ca

Cover and interior design by John Luckhurst
Images courtesy Dawn Vaessen
Map on page 13 published by Natural Resources Canada (Canadian Forest Service) and Agriculture and Agri-Food Canada. Reproduced with the permission of Natural Resources Canada, Canadian Forest Service.

Printed and bound in Hong Kong, China.

1 3 5 7 9 10 8 6 4 2

Library and Archives Canada Cataloguing in Publication

Vaessen, Dawn, 1972-
Perfect perennials for the prairie gardener / Dawn Vaessen.
Includes index.
ISBN 978-1-897252-51-2
1. Perennials—Prairie Provinces. 2. Gardening—Prairie
Provinces. I. Title.

SB434.V33 2010   635.9'3209712   C2010-902241-6

Fifth House Ltd. gratefully acknowledges the support of the Canada Council for the Arts, the Department of Canadian Heritage and the Ontario Arts Council. We acknowledge the financial support of the Government of Canada through the Canada Book Fund for our publishing program.

Page 13: Canadian plant hardiness zone map. Published by Natural Resources Canada (Canadian Forest Service) and Agriculture and Agri-Food Canada. Reproduced with the permission of Natural Resources Canada, Canadian Forest Service.

Page vi: Excerpt of lyrics from the song, "Lonely Love," from the album La De Da (2005), written by Joel Plaskett. Reproduced with the permission of Joel Plaskett.

Contents

To my mom and
gardening inspiration
Joyce Vaessen
and to my kids
Bryna and Sofie Turk

"Dirt under your nails
from working in the garden
trying to grow a plant
With the wind under our sails
You and I were gettin' started
don't tell me that you can't"

LONELY LOVE FROM LADEDA
BY CANADIAN FOLK ARTIST
JOEL PLASKETT (2005)

Acknowledgements

I'm often asked how I managed to write a book while working fulltime and having a young family. The answer is, I'm not really sure, but it could never have happened if it weren't for the following people.

I would like to thank the following people who have developed and fuelled my love of perennial gardening. At the top of the list are gardening gurus Jeff De Jong and Jane Reksten who taught me so much about prairie perennial gardening. Through the thoroughly informative and entertaining Master Gardener course they taught at the Calgary Zoo, I learned to work with my garden instead of battling against it. Sara Williams's books on prairie growing have been immensely informative, too, and it was after hearing her speak that I was inspired to send in my idea for a gardening book. Fran and Connell Minty of Namaka Ridge Tree Farm near Strathmore, AB, were so supportive of my work and encouraged me to try my hand at developing a perennial workshop that they so kindly hosted. Thanks so much!

Thanks also to Charlene Dobmeier of Kinglsey Publishing and Stephanie Stewart of Fifth House Publishers for believing in my ideas and making my dream of writing a book come true. Kristen and Meaghan Craven, the word goddesses, for editing and reediting my work to make it the best it could be, also deserve a big thank you. Thanks also to Winston Goretsky for helping me out with pictures when I was in a bind. He truly is a "great one."

I cannot thank my friends and family enough for their support. The "Saturday Gardeners," including Kelly, Fran, Kim, and Karen; Diana, the only one who "gets" me; and Curtis, the marketing wizard, have helped me in ways that cannot be measured. My friends, listed and unlisted, are the best and I love them all. My toughest audience has always been the students I teach, especially those from St. Gabriel in Chestermere, AB, and St. Martha in Calgary. They have encouraged me "not to make it boring in a way that teachers often do" and I hope I didn't disappoint. My Grandma is the reason I developed a love of books, and her spirit has guided me throughout this one's development. To my parents, Norbert and Joyce, sister Tracy and brother Preston: You are amazing, are my biggest support, and I could not have done any of this without you. And to my kids Bryna and Sofie Turk, whom I will love forever. Thank you, thank you, thank you!

CHAPTER ONE

What's a Perennial Anyway?

Ah, the garden. It's the only place where big tacky flowers are tasteful, and it's perfectly acceptable to design with plastic gnomes. While gardening sounds like it should be a lot of fun and enjoyment, for many it's a source of frustration and something that is just plain perplexing. Though many people may want to develop gardens around their prairie dwellings, they can quickly become confused and frustrated by the limitations on growing this region presents. People may quip, "Does anything grow here, and if so, how do you develop a garden on the Prairies?" The following pages seek to dispel the myth that prairie gardening is an oxymoron at best. Before a list of perennials is perused, it's important to get down to the nitty-gritty and define what a perennial is, who "Saturday gardeners" are, and demystify all of the Latin terminology used when plant people "talk shop." Once definitions are learned and the basics laid out, it's easier to understand perennials and know just what you're looking for when developing your own backyard retreat.

A Straightforward Definition

My friend Karen once asked me, "So, what's a perennial anyway?" While experienced green thumbs assume everyone knows the answer to this question, new gardeners may not. A perennial, simply stated, is a plant that comes to life in the garden three or more spring seasons in a row. Plants sold as annuals last one growing season and usually die after the first hard frost of fall or if someone forgets to water it during summer vacation. Perennials are tougher and generally require less care than annual bedding plants.

Several types of perennial plants can exist and do quite well in prairie gardens. They may be herbaceous (dying to the ground every fall), or evergreen (keeping their leaves green even in winter). Some perennials, like the honeysuckle vine, even have stems similar to the woody branches of trees and shrubs and pop out buds in the spring on this existing wood.

Perennials come in a variety of shapes, sizes, colours, and textures. Different perennials emerge at different times throughout the spring. For example, while some sedums look alive in March, plants like hostas may not appear until early June. Though perennials offer a lot of diversity in terms of size, colour, and foliage, they all help to make the garden look lush and alive. No prairie garden is complete without a variety of hardy perennial plantings. Perennials also differ in how long they're able to live in the garden. While plants like peonies have a lifespan longer than the average human, some perennials, like pinks, will only live for a couple of years. Knowing a perennial's lifespan is important if you want it to continue having a long-term spot in your gardening space.

Often confused with perennials, biennials are plants that require two growing seasons in order to complete their life cycle. Typically, biennials grow leaves their first year, and then flower and set seeds the second year. Though biennials have a short lifespan, many tend to self-seed every year. Hollyhocks are an example of a successful prairie biennial.

Prairie-hardy perennials are a good choice for anyone wishing to add colour and texture to their yard. The perennials in this book are easy to take care of and don't require a lot of attention once established—a plus for those who don't want to become slaves to their gardens. While they don't bloom as long as annuals do (some lasting only a few weeks), it's possible to have continuous colour in a prairie garden throughout its short growing season. All that's needed is a bit of planning and a list of prairie-hardy plants. These perennials don't require the watering many annuals do, and are well suited to the prairie climate. Many of the choices listed in this book are resistant to drought and the heat of a prairie summer, and all of them are capable of surviving the Prairie's crazy cold winters. These plants are resilient but also add a lot of landscape appeal. While others may view the Prairies as Canada's hinterland, it's important for prairie gardeners to keep an open mind and focus on what we can grow, and not on what we can't. Surprisingly, we can grow a lot, and it can look great, too.

The Typical "Saturday Gardener"

This book is targeted at prairie people who want to grow plants but have no idea about where to begin. As every new resident of the Prairies knows, just living here can be harsh. An outsider need only imagine how difficult it is to successfully grow plants if the thought of minus-forty-degree weather causes cringing. Many books that approach Canadian gardening, unfortunately, focus on conditions experienced in southern Ontario or British Columbia. This is a pipe dream for prairie residents, as we can't grow the same plants other people do in other parts of the country. Though challenging, prairie gardening is not impossible. Growing plants here is a more severe task than in the rest of Canada (considering our short growing season and cold climate), but it's not always harder in terms of labour, time, and maintenance. Knowing and accepting the reality of this region is the first step in developing a great garden.

There are a lot of "Saturday gardeners" on the Prairies, and I know this because I used to be one. Saturday gardeners aren't usually hard core about growing plants, but they still want to experience gardening success, albeit using the least amount of effort. They don't typically read gardening magazines, or know the Latin names of plants. Come spring, however, Saturday gardeners suddenly emerge from hiding. Hordes of people flock to garden centres with the hope of creating a fantastic landscape that will wow their friends during barbeque season. Saturday gardeners make up the majority of this bunch who seek to recreate Eden in their backyards. Money is spent on all sorts of plants, pots, and ornaments to add instant impact to the yard. Unfortunately, when summer hits, the dream for many has all but faded, and many of the plants have been junked.

Master Gardener Programs on the Prairies

If you want to know more about gardening in your specific area, a master gardener program is a great place to start. Each program is region- or area-specific and is geared toward everyone from the gardening clueless to the advanced green thumb. The knowledge I acquired through the master gardener program was the deciding factor in making my garden go from gross to glorious. Here is some information about the master gardener programs offered across the Canadian Prairies:

◆ **The University of Saskatchewan Master Gardener Program**
includes two streams: core educational courses (some offered through distance education), and special interest workshops (held across the province). The only prerequisite is a desire to grow:

University of Saskatchewan Master Gardener Program
Centre for Continuing & Distance Education
Room 477 Williams Building, 221 Cumberland Avenue North
Saskatoon, SK S7N 1M3
E-mail: master.gardeners@usask.ca
Web site: http://www.ccde.usask.ca/mastergardener/contact

◆ **The Devonian Botanic Garden Master Gardener Program**
is a site-based course open to residents of Edmonton, Alberta. The course runs from September to April, once a week. Applications are required for the course:

Adult Education
Devonian Botanic Garden
University of Alberta
Edmonton, AB T6G 2E1
E-mail: DBGeducation@ales.ualberta.ca
Web site: http://www.devonian.ales.ualberta.ca/master_gardener.cfm

◆ **The Calgary Zoo's Master Gardener Training Program**
offers specific information for growing plants in the Chinook zone. The course runs weekly from November to April. The Woody Plant ID course is a prerequisite:

Calgary Zoo, Botanical Garden & Prehistoric Park
13400 Zoo Road Northeast
Calgary, AB T2E 7V6
E-mail: janer@calgaryzoo.ab.ca
Web site: http://www.calgaryzoo.org

While experienced gardeners know what they're looking for and have a plan for planting, many beginners don't. They look at the long rows of new plants adorning the garden centre aisles and think, "What is it I want again?" Beginning and veteran gardeners typically want the same result for their yards: plants that look great, survive prairie winters, and need little maintenance. Every April I have requests from friends to help prepare their backyard beds. The same question pops up again and again when I talk to my buddies about planting their plots: What do you do first? The problem for nongardeners is not a lack of enthusiasm. Rather, they don't have any idea of where to begin.

Like I said, I used to be a Saturday gardener. I would blindly go to garden centres during the May long weekend, purchasing plants that looked nice on the tags. I bought according to the colour on the label, and by flower type (daisy-shaped, rose-like, etc.), with little regard for planting zone, size, shape, or leaf texture. Once summer hit, I'd look at my backyard and think, "Why isn't my garden working?" Something wasn't right. My stretch of plants didn't resemble the mental image I'd created back in May. I decided to investigate why my perennials were disappointing me.

Resolved to learn more about creating the garden space I craved, I read everything I could about growing on the Canadian Prairies. I also took the Master Gardener Training Program through the Calgary Zoo. Through these classes, I learned that establishing the lush garden I dreamed of was not an impossible task, and that building my garden would be easier than I had previously thought. What I needed to change was the way I did things and not the amount of time and labour I'd been investing in gardening. The most important thing I learned about gardening is that the right plants need to be planted in the right locations. While this seems like a no-brainer, many people fail to remember this when digging in spring perennials. The focus of the following pages is to determine and find the perfect prairie plants for the ideal garden spot.

Botanical Lingo

New gardeners may ask, "What's with all the Latin names anyway?" Many people get intimidated or sneer when experienced green thumbs use Latin or botanical names for plant identification. Throughout the book, perennials are listed by both their common and botanical names. The botanical naming system is actually not as hard to understand as many people think, and once its purpose is understood, the botanical terms actually make sense.

There are several reasons why botanical names are useful to gardeners. Latin is a universal language that is used to denote both the genus and species of a plant. This ensures it can be identified in spite of having many common names. The perennial *Liatris spicata* is a good example. It's known by the names 'Gay feather' and 'Blazing Star.' Knowing the plant's genus and species can help you avoid confusion at the garden centre if you know the plant by another name than that given on the plant's tag. Botanical names also help distinguish dissimilar plants that may have the same common name. Though *Bergenia cordifolia* is often referred to as elephant ears, there are other plant species that share this name (including ligularia). Knowing botanical

Botanical Plant Terminology

Have you ever wondered what the different labels, symbols, or names mean on the plant tags you buy? The chart below explains the components of a plant's botanical name and defines commonly used greenhouse descriptions or terms.

Term	Definition and Importance	Example (in red)
Genus	A group of closely related plants.	*Iris sibirica* (Siberian iris)
Species	Individual plants that are able to successfully breed together from one generation to the next. When referring to a plant species in a broad context, "sp." is used.	*Echinacea purpurea* (purple coneflower)
Cultivar/Variety	Refers to "cultivated variety." These plants have been selectively grown based on certain characteristics that make them desirable. Several cultivars may exist within a given plant species.	*Lysimachia punctata* 'Alexander' (variegated yellow loosestrife)
Hybrid	A plant that is a cross between two different species. Hybrids are identified with an "x" and don't usually produce viable seeds.	*Calamagrostis x acutiflora* (feather reed grass)
Specific Epithet	A descriptive word or term used in distinguishing one species or cultivar from another. It is the second part of the botanical name. The word by itself may mean little, but when combined with the genus, it becomes the botanical name of the species.	*Dianthus deltoides* (maiden pinks)

names may save you money and frustration later on, and help you to avoid buying unwanted plants.

Botanical classification can also identify closely related plants of the same genus. While these plants may not look alike, they may thrive in similar growing conditions. Two plants that fit this description are *Lysimachia punctata* 'Alexander' (variegated yellow loosestrife) and *Lysimachia nummularia* 'Aurea' (golden creeping Jenny). These two perennials look nothing alike, but belonging to the same genus means they share similar characteristics that separate them from other groups of plants—in this case, moist, partly sunny garden spots.

CHAPTER TWO

The Prairie Gardening Reality

The truth of gardening on the Prairies is that we have a really short growing time and our perennials must endure extreme weather conditions in every season. That said, gardening can be a successful venture that's also a lot of fun. The key is in knowing what you are dealing with. This means accepting the fact that snow can appear on the Prairies in June and hailstorms will hit at any time. Plant hardiness zones, too, must be acknowledged by prairie gardeners. If they're ignored, time and money can be wasted on perennials that simply won't thrive. Next, there are soil conditions to worry about, including knowing the "flavour" of the dirt you're dealing with and how this will affect your plants. If you're prepared for prairie gardening conditions, then developing a perennial garden will be a snap.

The Prairie Climate

The environment has steadily become a concern for all Canadians. As prairie residents, many of our livelihoods, or those of people we know, are tied to climatic patterns and weather. On the Prairies, the climate is often highly variable from year to year. Summers are turning cooler and winters warmer. The climate is changing and not necessarily for the better. Climatic change has a direct impact not only on the topics of conversation discussed at the local coffee shop but also on the plant choices that need to be made. On the Prairies, we're limited in terms of what plants will grow successfully. Are we to toss up our hands in defeat and strictly grow potentillas and junipers (commonly referred to as "gas station plants" since they require very little attention)? Not exactly, but it does mean that gardeners have to plan their choices with care.

On the bright side, there are many great perennials for prairie dwellers. Successful planting, however, is dependent upon realizing that gardening in this region is very different than in other areas of Canada. Growing plants that are adapted to the climates of Ontario and British Columbia won't necessarily work in Manitoba, Saskatchewan, and Alberta. Prairie gardeners know that it's important to work with what you have, and not with what you wish to have, and they accept the fact that violent hailstorms and periods of drought will occur. It's not a matter of *if* these things will happen, but when, and with what severity. Knowing the reality of the prairie region is key and, unfortunately, too many enthusiastic Saturday gardeners buy plants first and ask questions later. Part of the secret to successful planting is in realizing what you have, and working with it to the best of your ability. Working against it, however, will result in disappointment, money lost, and unhappy plants. In other words, investigate your planting area well before you start filling it with greenery.

Top Web Sites for Prairie Gardeners

◆ http://www.umanitoba.ca/afs/hort_inquiries/
The University of Manitoba Plant Sciences Horticultural Inquiries Web site offers easy-to-follow information about prairie plant conundrums.

◆ http://www.planthardiness.gc.ca
Canada's Plant Hardiness Site—Going Beyond the Zones (Natural Resources Canada) is a government Web site that gives gardeners a list of plants that are able to survive in different areas of the country.

◆ http://www.gardenline.usask.ca
This is a great Web site from the University of Saskatchewan Extension Division that offers prairie growers a wealth of information on everything from tough perennials to lawn care.

◆ http://www.calhort.org
The Calgary Horticultural Society's Web site offers everything needed to garden in Alberta's Chinook zone and useful information for all prairie residents.

◆ http://www.wildaboutgardening.org
Sponsored by the Canadian Wildlife Federation, this funky site offers tips on eco-gardening and growing in small spaces.

◆ http://www.extension.umn.edu/GardenInfo
This is a University of Minnesota Extension Web site that offers a range of gardening information, including sections called, "What's Wrong with My Plant?" and "Is This Plant a Weed?"

Microclimates

Before anything is planted, the microclimate of your garden has to be determined. A microclimate is the unique and specific growing reality experienced in an individual landscape or yard. Microclimates are determined by assessing the structures, site locations of garden beds, and sun exposure that exist in your yard. Knowing your microclimate will impact the plant varieties that will successfully grow in your garden. A very sheltered microclimate will be more favourable for many perennials than an exposed area without windbreaks and structures. So how is this determined, you may ask? The following is a list of questions that need to be answered in determining the microclimate of a yard:

◆ What direction do the garden beds face?
◆ How much sun (in hours) does the garden receive on a daily basis?
◆ Is the site hot and dry, or is it shaded and moist?
◆ Are there any areas that don't receive breezes or wind?
◆ Is the garden space sheltered by structures, trees, and fences, or is it exposed?

Knowing your microclimate can save you money and heartbreak in the long run. You'll also develop an idea of which plant types will work in your yard, and which ones simply will not.

Hailstorms

Hail will happen. The question isn't if or maybe, but when. It's a hard reality of living where we do, but it has to be addressed. I shudder to remember how one of my big beautiful hostas looked after two minutes of fierce marble-sized hail. I had, just days before, repositioned the beauty to the perfect spot. If only I'd known what was to come. After the brief storm, it looked like a sociopath had taken scissors and meticulously cut through every chartreuse leaf. When the same thing happened the following year, I moved the hosta and accepted the fact that hail happens, and I couldn't change that fact. It only takes a few seconds of hail pellets to level a season of growth and hard work.

While you may be thinking that all hope is lost, it's not. There are a few plants that offer hail resistance and adapt quite well to prairie living. Perennials with fine-textured leaves, including grasses and day lilies, do a great job of repelling hailstone damage. Sedum, too, bounces back after storms hit, though the thick fleshy leaves may be pockmarked. Using hail-resistant plants in exposed beds is a good option for anyone living on the Prairies.

Hail-Resistant Perennial Choices (Foliage Only)
◆ blazing star (*Liatris spicata*)
◆ blue fescue grass (*Festuca glauca*)
◆ pinks (*Dianthus gratianopolitanus, D. deltoides*)
◆ day lily (*Hemerocallis* sp.)
◆ feather reed grass 'Karl Foerster' (*Calamagrostis* x *acutiflora* 'Karl Foerster')
◆ moss phlox (*Phlox subulata*)
◆ Siberian iris (*Iris sibirica*)
◆ stonecrop (*Sedum* sp.)
◆ thrift (*Armeria maritima*)

Drought

Drought, too, is a hard prairie truth. Who hasn't been slightly annoyed by idiots in August who spout off the clichéd, "hot enough fer ya?" On the Prairies, we know heat like we know cold. Because of this, a selection of drought-tolerant perennials should exist in every prairie garden. Many plants listed in this book are sun-loving and drought-tolerant. Plants like sedum and hens and chicks actually do quite well in the heat, and with limited water. In the near future, water restrictions will become a reality in many prairie communities both small and large. Therefore, sun-loving, drought-resistant perennials are a must for regional residents. Below is a list of the garden superheroes in the prairie heat.

Drought tolerant plants like this lamb's ear often have
fuzzy textures that aid in capturing air-borne moisture.

Drought-Tolerant Perennial Choices
- bigroot cranesbill geranium (*Geranium macrorrhizum*)
- blanket flower (*Gaillardia* x *grandiflora*)
- blazing star (*Liatris spicata*)
- blue fescue grass (*Festuca glauca*)
- cheddar pinks (*Dianthus gratianopolitanus*)
- cushion spurge (*Euphorbia polychroma*)
- day lily (*Hemerocallis* sp.)
- elephant ears (*Bergenia cordifolia*)
- lamb's ear (*Stachys byzantina*)
- sage (*Salvia* x *sylvestris*)
- Siberian iris (*Iris sibirica*)
- thrift (*Armeria maritima*)
- woolly thyme (*Thymus pseudolanuginosus*)

Growing Days

When I moved to Calgary, Alberta, after graduating university, I was eager to begin gardening. Why wouldn't I have been? The gardening was definitely going to be better in balmy Calgary than it was in frigid Saskatoon, Saskatchewan, right? My perception, however, was skewed. Attempts at recreating my mother's lush garden in small-town Saskatchewan were dismal. My plants were small and puny compared to similar types my friends and family grew near Saskatoon. What was I doing wrong? After looking into things, it turns out it wasn't me but the growing days Calgary experiences.

Every plant needs a predetermined number of "growing degree days" in order to develop and reach its full potential. This refers to the number of days a plant needs in order to reach maturity and bloom. Growing days are estimates used by greenhouse operators and gardeners to estimate the date at which a plant will reach its full potential. A "growing day" can be any day where the high doesn't reach above 30°C (plants tend not to grow when it gets this hot out) and doesn't fall below 5°C (plants stop growing when it's this cold).

Growing Days vs. Growing Degree Days

A "growing degree day" is different than a "growing day" and is the average of the maximum and minimum temperature in a day minus a base temperature below which plants do not grow. There is an upper and lower temperature at which many plants stop growing. It's convenient to use 30°C as an upper temperature and 5°C as a base temperature on the Prairies. For example, on a day where the high was 23°C and the low was 10°C, we could say: $(23 + 10)/2 - 5 = 11.5$. Thus, 11.5 degree days were contributed that day. Each plant needs its own number of degree days to become what it's expected to be.

While there is much variation among species, on average, plants need a minimum temperature of 5°C to 7°C to grow. This explained my puny plants; they simply weren't receiving the same number of growing days the Saskatoon plants were. Calgary, being close to the Rockies, has a much higher altitude, and therefore cooler average temperatures, than other places on the Prairies. It gets downright chilly at night, and every Calgarian knows that a jacket is often required for an evening stroll in June. Since plants continue to grow at night if the conditions are right, some prairie places have more growing days than others. One estimate I heard was that Edmonton received forty-two more growing degree days than Calgary in an average year! This explains why people living in Calgary have such a difficult time successfully growing tomatoes outdoors compared to other prairie inhabitants. While it's hard to grow tomatoes and peppers successfully, being close to the mountains means that growing alpine plants like saxifrage is a breeze. Being aware of the local landscape in terms of latitude, climate, altitude, and topography can help in determining what will grow successfully in your yard, and what will be a struggle.

What's Your Zone?

One day I was out running with my friend Adrienne. It was -20°C, I was four kilometres into the run with another three to go, and I had to do something to take my mind off the stabbing pain I felt in my lungs. As a diversion, and in an attempt to keep pace with the fit and bubbly Adrienne, I started talking about the glowing red dogwood shrubs that adorned the winter pathway. "Oh," she said without any huffing or puffing, "I never noticed those before, but they're kind of nice." Adrienne then proceeded to proudly talk plants with me, and began mentioning the tulip bulbs she planted in the fall. "They're going to be so beautiful . . . I just can't wait," she spouted. Gasping, I responded, "Hope they're the right zone . . . sometimes the bulbs . . . available at the . . . chain stores . . . don't adapt . . . that well to . . . Calgary's climate."

It took me a long time to get that out, but I forgot my exhausted state for a moment. "Zone?" Adrienne replied, "What do you mean by zone?" I then proceeded to explain the plant hardiness zones of Canada to my perplexed running mate. "No one told me about these zones," Adrienne asserted. "Why didn't they let me know that when I bought them? They were so pretty on the box." My friend looked both puzzled and shocked. Poor Adrienne. Wasn't it better that she learn the cold, hard truth about zones sooner than later?

In 2000, Agriculture Canada released an updated version of its Plant Hardiness Map of Canada. The map breaks the country up into nine zones where plants, including trees, shrubs, and perennials, are able to consistently survive winters. These zones range from zero to eight, with zero representing northern latitudes and eight representing the extreme southwest region of British Columbia. The zones are based on various climatic variables, including average January temperatures, snowfall, and wind speed. This may seem boring and unimportant, but it's vital when choosing plants that will thrive in your garden space. Knowing your zone and the plants that are well adapted to it will save you time, money, and high levels of frustration in the long run.

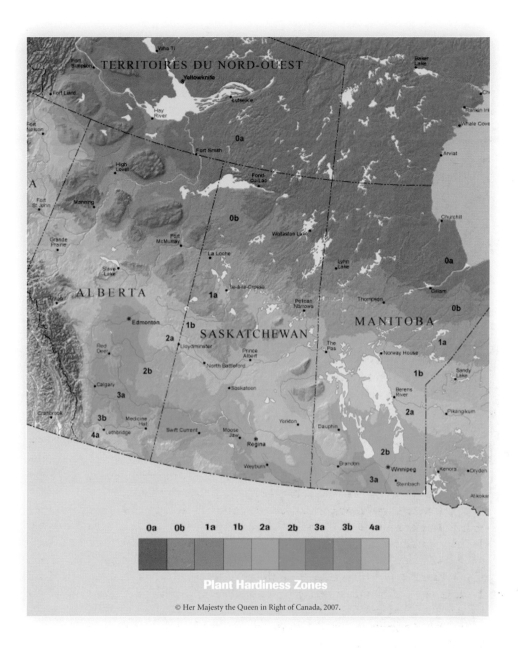

Why Are Zones Vital?

A variety of plant hardiness zones exist on the Prairies. Prairie zones range from 2A to 4A. On plant tags in garden centres, you may notice a distinction between zones with the labels "A" or "B." The designation of "A" or "B" is based on slight variations in climatic harshness within a zoned region. Regina, Saskatchewan, for example is in zone 2B, while North Battleford, Saskatchewan, is in zone 2A. On average, North Battleford's climatic conditions, local landscape, and exposure to winter weather is slightly harsher than that of Regina's. While this discrepancy exists, don't let it stop you from purchasing a zone 3B plant you love if you live in zone 3A. Seasoned gardeners are always "pushing the zone," or planting perennials that don't always grow with a definite zoning guarantee. The perennial lamb's ear is often listed as zone 4, though it does well in my 3A garden. A quick look at the plant tags at your local garden centre will tell you the zone each plant will consistently survive in. Knowing your garden's zone and those of particular plants will prevent wasted time, money loss, and frustration in the long run.

Soil vs. Dirt

One spring day in the staff room of the school I was teaching at, my colleague Monica was regaling her experience buying supplies at a local gardening centre. While many of the teachers were leisurely enjoying a student-free lunch, an incensed Monica started her tale for all of us to hear.

She was on a quest to make her flower bed beautiful, but she needed help in accomplishing her goal. Upon finding a sales associate at the gardening centre, she quipped how she required some dirt for her new plants. An unnerving silence fell over the entire place, and a purse-lipped and sober attendant replied, "We do *not* sell dirt here. We sell soil!" Monica's jaw dropped. She couldn't believe the attendant's pompous behaviour and was slightly disturbed by this reaction to her simple request.

Dirt or soil: isn't it all the same stuff? Monica did have a point. Just as civil engineers cringe when lay people refer to concrete as "cement," many experienced gardeners detest precious soil being called "dirt." The term "soil" does have a nicer ring than lowly "dirt," but let's face it; we're all referring to the same stuff. Essentially, it all comes down to semantics when answering the question, "Is it dirt or is it soil?" What becomes important is not so much the name you give it but whether or not you know what type you're dealing with in your garden.

Soil Types

The composition of the soil you have in your yard is just as important as the location in which you plant. Soil is made up of air, water, rocks, minerals, and organic matter, including things dead and alive. There are three types of dirt that exist in a prairie gardener's soil: clay, silt, and sand. Depending on where you live, prairie soils may be more clay-based or more sand-based. All three types of dirt have benefits, as well as limitations. It's important to remember that your soil includes a combination of all three types of dirt listed below. The perfect combination of soil is known as loam, which includes equal parts of the three types with the added bonus of humus (dead organic stuff). Loamy soils offer high rates of fertility and hold water well, while at the same time offering decent drainage. It's the ideal "dirt" in which to grow things.

Clay-rich: This type of soil has an abundance of the smallest types of soil mineral particles. Heavy, clumpy, and poorly drained are good words to describe clay soils. Clay consists of tiny particles that stick like glue to each other when wet. When dried, clay forms big rock-hard clumps that are hard to break up. The problem with clay-rich soil is that it tends to become waterlogged, and during the winter this can become a problem for many plants. Since it doesn't easily drain, amendment is necessary if you have clay-rich soil. Amendment refers to digging in compost (the more the better), which is very important, as the humus or decomposed matter helps to break up the chunks and add nutrients that will benefit plants. Adding sand or even kitty litter (the cheap stuff works best) will help water drain away if clumpy clay soil is a problem. Much of the soil on the Prairies is clay-rich.

Silt-rich: These soil particles are smaller than sand but larger than clay. They're powdery to the touch and will easily slip through your fingers. Silt is commonly found along flood plains and is ideal for growing crops, though it easily erodes. Silt is the major soil component in creating mud.

Sand-rich: The largest among soil particles, sand feels gritty when squeezed. Sandy soil allows for quick drainage and doesn't offer much in terms of organic material. It tends to have lower fertility levels and lacks nutrients, so amending it with compost is a must. Sandy soils are prone to erosion as the particles don't clump together like clay.

You may be thinking this is all fine and dandy, but how do I find out what my soil is made up of? One method used for determining soil type is called the squeeze test. As described above, each of the soil types has a different composition and texture. When clay is squeezed, it feels sticky and has a doughy texture. When sand is squeezed, it feels gritty and loose. When silt is squeezed, it feels powdery and fine, similar to the texture of flour. Take a fistful of dirt and squeeze it if you're uncertain. If you can make a ball with your dirt, it's probably clay-based, and if you can't it's probably on the sandier side. Knowing this information about your backyard dirt will make tending to the needs of your individual plants a breeze.

The Flavour of Dirt

Though it may be hard to believe, your soil has a distinct flavour that will directly impact your plants. Dirt in your yard will have either an alkaline "taste," or one that is slightly more acidic, according to your perennials (it is unadvisable to try a soil taste test yourself, as it is full of critters and your neighbours will assume you're crazy, and believe me, they're watching). This soil alkalinity or acidity can be measured using a pH scale numbered from one to fourteen. The lower numbers represent extreme soil acidity, while the upper ones represent levels of high alkalinity. Different perennials tolerate different soil "flavours," so it's important to know what you're dealing with. Soil test kits are available at most major garden centres for home testing, and are inexpensive and easy to use.

Generally, prairie soils tend to be alkaline. While it's true that few plants adore heavy alkaline levels, there are a number of perennials that tolerate it. For extremely alkaline soils, the addition of compost will help lower the pH level of the soil, as acids are released during the process of decomposition. The more you dig in, the better. Once again, compost is the answer to another gardening conundrum.

Perennials for Alkaline Soil

- bergenia (*Bergenia cordifolia*)
- clematis (*Clematis* sp.)
- coral bells (*Heuchera* sp.)
- creeping baby's breath (*Gypsophila repens*)
- lamb's ear (*Stachys byzantina*)
- Maltese cross (*Lychnis chalcedonica*)
- peony (*Paeonia lactiflora*)
- pinks (*Dianthus gratianopolitanus* & *D. deltoides*)
- sage (*Salvia* x *sylvestris*)

Perennials for Poor Sandy Soils

- artemisia, 'Silver Brocade' (*Artemisia stelleriana*)
- creeping baby's breath (*Gypsophila repens*)
- globe thistle (*Echiops ritro*)
- hens and chicks (*Sempervivum* sp.)
- Iceland poppy (*Papaver nudicaule*)
- lamb's ear (*Stachys byzantina*)
- sage (*Salvia* x *sylvestris)*
- stonecrop (*Sedum* sp.)
- snow in summer (*Cerastium tomentosum*)
- thrift (*Armeria maritima*)
- woolly thyme (*Thymus pseudolanuginosus*)

Perennials for Heavy Clay Soils

- astilbe (*Astilbe* x *arendsii*)
- beebalm (*Monarda* hybrids)
- bergenia (*Bergenia cordifolia*)
- bigroot cranesbill geranium (*Geranium macrorrhizum*)
- blazing star (*Liatris spicata*)
- coneflower (*Echinacea purpurea*)
- coral bells (*Heuchera* sp.)
- day lily (*Hemerocallis* sp.)
- fernleaf bleeding heart (*Dicentra formosa*)
- hosta (*Hosta* sp.)
- ligularia (*Ligularia dentata*)
- Maltese cross (*Lychnis chalcedonica*)
- moss phlox (*Phlox subulata*)
- rudbeckia (*Rudbeckia fulgida* var. *sullivantii*)

CHAPTER THREE

What to Know Before Buying Perennials

So many of us trounce off to the garden centres with little consideration about what we're buying, where we're going to plant, and just what we're looking for in the first place. This chapter explores what is necessary before a trip to the garden store is warranted. Included is information on the elements of colour and texture in garden design, as well as tips on buying and planting the perfect perennials. Knowing what you want ahead of time will help prevent against rising frustration levels once you arrive to buy your plants.

The Importance of Colour and Texture in the Garden

Before I developed any notion of colour and placement theory in the garden, my beds were a mishmash of bloom tones with little existing order. I'd place perennials according to convenience (the closest available spot), rather than develop a planting plan that included texture and colour. Little did I realize that where a perennial is placed can make or break the appeal of a desired gardenscape.

Colour

Before you purchase plants, you should have some concept of the colours you want in your garden. Favourite colours reflect our personalities and show through in the flower choices we make. Reds, oranges, and yellows represent feelings of excitement and energy, and in the garden these colours tend to spring up at those who stroll by. Though they get noticed first, these colours also create the illusion of smallness. They should be used with caution if you have limited garden space. That said, hot colours add spark to the landscape. Cooler colours like blues, indigos, and purples, however, tend to denote calm and create feelings of relaxation. In the garden, these colours tend to recede into the landscape and make the garden seem bigger than it actually is. Do you want big, bold blooms to explode in the garden, or do you seek cool, soothing colours that produce tranquility? Thinking about what you want the colours in your garden to "say" says a lot about your personality and can help in deciding which perennials to include in the landscape. A little bit of colour-palette planning might be a determining factor in whether your garden is a personal triumph or a disorganized patchwork of blooms.

The colour wheel below will help in deciding which colours to include in your landscape. It's important to plan your colour combinations before you go out and buy plants. This would include both complementary and analogous colour blends. Complementary colours on the colour wheel are those that are directly opposite one another, like red and green. The rule of thumb is if you want to show off a particular bloom colour, you plant it beside its opposite. However contradictory this may sound, it really does work. My favourite colour is red, so for my crimson flowers I include a lot of contrasting green foliage close by. While this rule goes against any fashion rules that may exist beyond your fence, in your garden it works like a charm.

Planting analogous colours together also works well. These include blooms with colours near one another on the colour wheel. For example, red, orange, and yellow are all analogous colours. It's important to remember that a successful garden includes both complementary and analogous colour schemes. Find what you like best, and work with it.

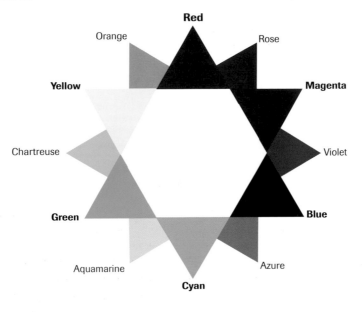

Texture

The term "texture" refers to the type of foliage or leaf structure of a plant. A good garden includes plants grown for their leaf texture and colour, as well as bloom type. The idea of contrasts works with texture as it does with colour. If you seek to show off a certain plant, place it near its opposite. Fine-textured grassy foliage stands out when it's placed alongside big brutish leaves. Varying types of texture should be a part of every garden, and opposites paired together create a stunning effect.

Not everything in the garden has to bloom. It's just as important to include plants that provide textural interest, as well as those with lots of colour. Foliage colour can be anything from yellowish-green to bluish-green, to purplish-red. The colour wheel principles apply with foliage as well as with blooms. Big green leaves do a fantastic job of showing off your red blooms. Incorporating foliage in your garden will make it appear lush and full as it matures.

While planting opposites is vital, it's equally important to include similar foliage types throughout your garden space. Fine-textured ornamental grass like 'Karl Foerster' can look out of place and awkward if it's the only grassy type in the landscape. Other grass-types repeated in the garden, such as the Siberian iris and day lily, complement 'Karl Foerster' grass nicely. This way, contrasting foliage won't stick out like a sore thumb and will blend in beautifully with the surroundings.

Perennials with Great Foliage
- artemisia (*Artemisia* sp.)
- astilbe (*Astilbe* x *arendsii*)
- bergenia (*Bergenia cordifolia*)
- blue fescue ornamental grass (*Festuca glauca*)
- coral bells (*Heuchera* sp.)
- day lily (*Hemerocallis* sp.)
- feather reed ornamental grass 'Karl Foerster' (*Calamagrostis acutiflora* 'Karl Foerster')
- hens and chicks (*Sempervivum* sp.)
- hosta (*Hosta* sp.)
- lamb's ear (*Stachys byzantina*)
- ligularia (*Ligularia* sp.)
- Siberian iris (*Iris sibirica*)
- stonecrop (*Sedum* sp.)

Where to Plant?

This is a question that plagues every gardener at some point; where do you put the plants you just bought? Too many times I've excitedly purchased plants that thrilled me in the store, only to think on the way home, "Oh yeah . . . where am I going to put this anyway?" The good news is that if you know your yard, then planting isn't really all that difficult. As previously mentioned, every yard has a microclimate. My yard's microclimate is the reason why I have a zone 4 lily growing in one very special sheltered location. Is it possible to plant fussier plants (anything listed as zone 4 or higher) throughout a backyard garden? No, but shelter, backdrops that support plants, and the degree of sun exposure go a long way in deciding what you can plant in your garden.

Sun Exposure

Not every part of your yard receives the same amount of sunlight. Sun exposure is affected by structures including fences, sheds, and other big buildings like houses. Take note of how much sun your backyard beds receive. Do plants get morning, afternoon, or evening sun? Are beds near any reflective surfaces that may give perennials some additional sizzle to deal with if it's hot out? If you're only thinking of these things after you've purchased your plants, just take note of where you sunbathe in the backyard and where you keep the ice bucket full of cold beverages. The answers to these questions will tell you where the full-sun spots are and where you can place your shade-loving plants. The lists below provide examples of perennials to plant in full sun, part sun, part shade, and full or dappled shade.

Plants for Full Sun (over six hours of sun)
- artemisia (*Artemisia* sp.)
- blanket flower (*Gaillardia* x *grandiflora*)
- blazing star (*Liatris spicata*)
- blue fescue ornamental grass (*Festuca glauca*)
- creeping baby's breath (*Gypsophila repens*)
- cushion spurge (*Euphorbia polychroma*)
- day lily (*Hemerocallis* sp.)
- feather reed ornamental grass, 'Karl Foerster' (*Calamagrostis acutiflora* 'Karl Foerster')
- globe thistle (*Echinops ritro*)
- hens and chicks (*Sempervivum* sp.)
- hollyhock (*Alcea rosea*)
- honeysuckle vine 'Dropmore scarlet' (*Lonicera* x *brownii* 'Dropmore scarlet')
- lamb's ear (*Stachys byzantina*)
- Maltese cross (*Lychnis chalcedonica*)
- pasque flower (*Pulsatilla vulgaris*)
- pussytoes (*Antennaria rosea*)
- rose campion (*Lychnis coronaria*)
- sage (*Salvia* x *sylvestris*)
- snow in summer (*Cerastium tomentosum*)
- stonecrop (*Sedum* sp.)
- thrift (*Armeria maritima*)
- woolly thyme (*Thymus pseudolanuginosus*)

Plants for Part Sun (four to six hours of sun)
- Asiatic lily (*Lilium* hybrids)
- beebalm (*Monarda* hybrids)
- clematis (*Clematis* sp.)
- coneflower (*Echinacea purpurea*)
- cranesbill: bigroot cranesbill geranium (*Geranium macrorrhizum*)
- moss phlox (*Phlox subulata*)
- peachleaf bellflower (*Campanula persicifolia*)
- pinks (*Dianthus gratianopolitanus* & *D. deltoides*)
- rudbeckia (*Rudbeckia fulgida* var. sullivantii)
- Siberian iris (*Iris sibirica*)
- yellow loosestrife (*Lysimachia punctata*)

Plants for Part Shade (two to four hours of sun)
- bergenia (*Bergenia cordifolia*)
- coral bells (*Heuchera* sp.)
- golden creeping Jenny (*Lysimachia nummularia* 'Aurea')
- hosta (light-coloured types) (*Hosta* sp.)
- periwinkle (*Vinca minor*)
- saxifrage (*Saxifraga paniculata*)

Plants for Full or Dappled Shade (less than two hours of sun per day)
- astilbe (*Asilbe* x *arendsii*)
- bergenia (*Bergenia cordifolia*)
- hosta (*Hosta* sp.)
- lamium (*Lamium maculatum*)
- ligularia (*Ligularia* sp.)
- Siberian bugloss (*Brunnera macrophylla*)

Buying and Choosing Perennials

While all gardeners are eager to head out to buy plants in the spring, Saturday gardeners are often hesitant upon entering a greenhouse for the first time. Which greenhouse is the best to buy from? Do I stroll the aisles, or do I stick to a mental list of flowers I want . . . and what exactly is it that I want again? These are questions we have all asked at some point in the gardening journey. A trip to the greenhouse doesn't have to be a source of frustration or bewilderment, if you know what you're looking for.

Friends often ask me where I like to buy my plants, and my response is the place with the best deals in May and June. In early spring, I try not to favour greenhouses over big-box stores, because at this point they're selling the same product. Once the growing season progresses, my opinion tends to change. While big-box stores may have good deals toward the end of the season, plants may not be consistently cared for. They may be suffering within the confines of their plastic containers due to infrequent watering and attention. Although plants may be cheaper to buy as the growing season wears on, they may also be sick and weak from overgrowth and stress. Greenhouses tend to their perennials in a consistent, thorough manner. Greenhouse staff know their stuff and do their best to ensure that the least amount of stress possible encroaches upon potted plants. If you must buy plants during the summer, a professionally staffed greenhouse might be your best bet.

All in all, I've had bad luck buying perennials in August and September. Though the deals are great, you may be buying puny plants that fail to emerge in the spring. Buying plants late in the growing season means that they don't have as much time to develop a strong root system that will ensure their winter survival. The earlier you buy potted perennials, the better. If you wait too late for a good deal, you may end up being disappointed.

Signs of a Healthy Plant

So how do you tell a healthy plant from a sick one? It's pretty straightforward, really. Try to avoid plants that look yellow and spotted with thin, gangly shoots. The tallest plants aren't necessarily the best, either. Often, short, stocky plants will outperform their tall, spindly counterparts in a matter of weeks once firmly planted. Healthy plants will have bold colour, with no spots or yellowing. Their stems will be strong and erect with abundant leaf growth at the base. Choice plants will be free of any mosses or other growth in the container, and won't have overgrown roots creeping out of the drainage holes. Buying healthy, well-established plants means you're one step closer to developing the garden of your dreams.

Plants that sit in their plastic containers for extended periods of time develop overgrown root systems. This leads to a stressed-out plant that becomes weak and prone to developing disease.

Where and How to Buy Plants

Before going shopping, it's important to make up a list of the perennials you want to buy. Unfortunately, for me this is easier said than done, as I never follow my own advice. So, let me rephrase that advice: Have an idea of what you want to buy, but be flexible, as most people's lists change when they arrive at the greenhouse. There, now I sound much less like a hypocrite. Many ideal perennial choices are described in Chapter 6 and can help you narrow down your options, either before or during your shopping trip.

Whether or not you want to buy large or small potted perennials is a matter of choice. Large pots offer immediate impact but are sometimes triple the price of their smaller compatriots. If two to three plants are required for your landscape, buying a larger potted perennial may be beneficial. One large perennial may be easily divided into three smaller plants (depending on the type of plant, of course), and dividing one plant into three means all will be the same size and bloom colour. Meanwhile, smaller pots are much cheaper than larger ones and often adapt better to the harshness of being transplanted. Tiny potted perennials, however, can take a lot longer to catch up, especially with slower growers that are less vigorous, such as ligularias and hostas. Small or big, the choice is yours. Do you want instant impact with money being no object, or are you a cheapskate who is willing to be patient? Assess the purpose of your perennial choices, along with their growth rates, and then make the decision.

How Many Plants Do I Need?

One important thing I learned in taking the master gardener course was that arranging perennials in planned groups of three or five has much more of an impact than using single or double plantings. I had no idea about any of this prior to taking the course, but I couldn't believe the difference it made to how my garden looked. Odd-numbered plantings look much better than even arrangements in the garden. This doesn't mean that every perennial must be in a grouping of three or five. Varying the number and grouping of plants will break up any monotony and will result in a more natural look.

If instant impact is desired, purchasing multiple plants might be the way to go. For thrifty gardeners who wish to multiply their plant numbers, waiting for a plant's root system to establish itself and then dividing it is a reasonable choice.

Accent Plants

Accent plants serve as focal points in the garden and will draw attention to specific locations in the yard. Large, or uniquely textured, perennials often don't need to be planted en masse and make for great accent plants. Ligularia and 'Karl Foerster' ornamental reed grass are large perennials that work quite well as feature or accent plants in small urban or suburban settings. On farms or acreages, gardeners can get away with planting biggies in numbers of threes or fives, but in the city this is often not possible. It's okay and advisable to plant accent plants, especially if you're on a budget. One clump of purple coneflowers looks just as good if it appears alone as it does in an odd-numbered grouping. Just remember to place it beside its opposite if you really want to show it off. It's also important to vary spacing and plant groupings throughout the garden. This makes plants appear as if they have a natural placement, even though they may have been carefully planned.

While it may seem like there are many "rules" to follow in creating a garden that rocks, it's essential to plant what you like and feel is right for your space. For example, if you're like my sister and adore plants whose leaves you can ruffle, choose tactile perennials like hosta and lamb's ear. If you dream of living in Australia like my pal Roni, plant clematis and honeysuckle vine. Remember, you're the one who is going to be in your garden the most, so plant according to your own style. Get a feel for what works and then go with it!

CHAPTER FOUR

Digging in, Maintaining, and Watching Your Garden Grow

Once you've chosen and purchased the right perennials, what comes next? While you may have an idea about placement, you might be clueless about the perfect depth of hole each perennial needs, or how much water and food the plants require. Questions about planting, maintenance, and gardening tools are answered in this chapter, along with a discussion of the importance of eco-gardening and yard clean-up. Gardening isn't only about growing pretty plants. It also involves environmental awareness and a degree of stewardship of the earth. Doing your part for the environment in terms of composting and collecting rainwater are not only responsible green choices but your plants will love you for it in the end. When these practices become routine, it's amazing just how easy it is to be an eco-friendly gardener and significantly reduce your ecological footprint.

Essential Tools

Anyone who ventures to home and garden centres or gardening shops in the spring will be awed and overwhelmed by the variety of garden gadgets available. Rakes and hoes alone can take up one full aisle. I remember going to a popular garden store with my friend Kelly, who exclaimed, "I just want a hole digger!" as we stared at rows and rows of trowels. How do you know which tools to buy when establishing a garden space? Surprisingly, you don't have to buy every tool in the store. That said, there are five tools no gardener should be without: a good pair of gloves, a trowel, a pair of shears, a sturdy spade, and a hoe. If you choose wisely, your garden tools will last a long time, to boot (*buying* boots is optional, of course!).

The Gloves

Gloves are essential when gardening. Digging in dirt is hard on the hands and severely dries them out. Gloves work to protect your hands against contact with abrasive foliage, thorns, and other yucky things. Many types of garden gloves exist in funky styles and patterns. You're no longer limited to the floral cotton grandma-types, or the leather farmer gloves of old. Hand covers with bold colours, diverse fabrics, and tough yet pliable leathers are now readily available.

While personal taste is the ultimate deciding factor, there are a few key elements to consider when opting for a pair of gloves. First, make sure they're a comfortable fit.

They should be snug, not constricting, and sturdy without being clunky. You want gloves that will keep your hands protected when cleaning up the yard, but at same time allow for the grasping of small stems. Second, make sure that your gloves are water-resistant and easy to wash off. It's surprising how quickly they can become soaked and mucky after a Saturday morning in the backyard. The last thing you want is to take off an uncomfortable pair of gloves and search for another pair when you have limited gardening time. You want gloves that will rinse off easily and allow excess water to be quickly shaken off, without slowing you down. Gloves that are made out of a combination of neoprene and soft leather work well for this, although they're pricier than other kinds. In the end, if you choose a pair of gloves that are comfortable, and look good, you'll be apt to use them regularly, and your cuticles will thank you.

The Trowel

A good garden trowel is indispensable. It's a digger, a tamper, a shovel, and more. A trowel is needed for digging your plants out of retail plastic pots and into the land-scape. Though many types and styles exist, when it comes to trowels, only one is needed. Don't be fooled by so-called ergonomic types that cost more; you would have to be using a trowel for hours a day in order to see the benefits. Choose one with a sturdy yet comfortable handle. The tool should fit your hand, and be stainless steel (it will wash off easily and won't rust). If you like colourful handles, or pointy blades over rounded ones, go with it. In the end, if you like your trowel, you'll use it more. Though rusty in places, I still use the first trowel I bought over ten years ago, for less than five bucks.

The Shears

This is one tool that literally can be used every day in the backyard. Garden shears are used for cutting back perennials that have grown too big (most plants actually like being cut, and perform better when it's done), getting rid of dead flowers, and a host of other jobs. All shears are the same, right? Wrong! Unlike a trowel, it's wise to spend money on a pair of quality garden shears. Let's just say I've learned my lesson after being chintzy with shears. In the end, a Swiss-made pair with red handles has won my favour. After frequently being left out in the rain and snow for three years (by accident, of course), it's still making the cut. Typically, three types of blades exist in secateurs (a fancy word for "shears"). The first are bypass blades, which are, by far, the best choice for Saturday gardeners. Parrot and anvil blades crush all but very small stems, which weakens them and allows disease to enter the plant more easily. They're not advisable if a multipurpose pair of garden shears is needed. Bypass pruners, like regular scissors, make clean cuts that do minimal damage to plant stems. Many types of shears are available, everything from XXL sizes to those with swivel handles. Again, it's impor-tant not to skimp on shears or you'll be returning to the garden store year after year.

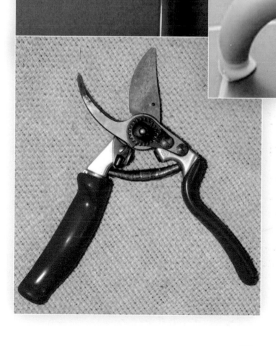

Garden tools come in an endless array of shapes, sizes and colours to choose from. Top centre: telescopic and pull-type hoes; Top inset: winged hoe for small spaces; Bottom right inset: ergonomic trowel to reduce hand strain; Bottom left: swivel-handled bypass pruners to prevent against tired hands.

BYPASS PRUNERS PHOTO BY WINSTON GORETSKY

The Spade

The spade is another valuable item you'll use again and again. A spade is a tool with a flat but sharp blade that's good for dividing perennials, as well as transferring small amounts of soil. Shovels, on the other hand, have curved and rounded blades that are ideal for digging holes. While the spade versus shovel debate could take up a whole chapter, it really comes down to personal preference when deciding which one you need. Before you buy, try out a few spades and shovels by handling them in the store. If the spade (or shovel) seems a good fit for your hands and the size is right, go for it. My own spade is 80 cm in length. For me, it's perfect for transferring soil or digging a hole, though it might not be if I were very tall. Like the trowel, only one is needed, so make sure it suits you well. A spade with a sharp edge works best. Each spring, all garden diggers (trowels included) should be sharpened in order to get the most out of your tool.

The Hoe

Hoes work best for turning soil and uprooting small annual weeds. Numerous styles and sizes are available, each serving its own purpose. Traditional pull hoes are best for overturning and chopping up patches of soil, while push-type Dutch hoes are ideal for weeding. Generally, long-handled hoes work best, but make sure the handle fits your height or excess stretching or bending may be required. Again, it all comes down to personal preference when choosing a hoe. My favourite is a winged variety that's shaped like a fighter jet. It's ideal for getting into small spaces and corners, and I wouldn't want to garden without it.

The Others

There are a few other items Saturday gardeners might find useful:

Velcro Tape: This is a great alternative to grandma's garden twine. Velcro strips can be cut to stake tall perennials and fix climbers to a trellis. Mildew-resistant and virtually indestructible, garden tape can be used again and again and camouflages well (it's usually a dull green colour).

Garden Knife: A small Swiss-type pocket knife is essential to have on hand for cutting tape and the like. My red-handled multipurpose knife works extremely well for this. In addition, it's effective for digging out perennial weeds with big roots like dandelions.

Trugs: A cross between a pail and a tub, trugs are extremely handy. They're useful in every task, from leaf-gathering to collecting water from downspouts. Available in various vibrant colours and sizes, no gardener should be without one.

Digging a Hole

A surprisingly common question I get from friends is how deep do you dig a hole for your plants? While it may seem simple enough, there are a few things to consider when digging in newly purchased perennials, including hole depth and methods of transplant. Once these are understood, digging is a snap.

Determining the Perfect Depth

Most perennials should be planted at the same level as they appear in their store-bought plastic containers. This means that the crowns of the plants are dug in at ground level. This rule doesn't apply to all perennials, though. Moisture-lovers like hostas should be planted with their crowns about 2-3 cm below ground level. Bearded irises benefit from a slightly raised position as their rhizomes will rot if planted too deep. When in doubt, check the planting instructions on the tag. They're there for a reason.

Transplanting and Establishing New Perennials

When it comes to perennials on the Prairies, the earlier you get them in the ground, the better. The major challenge of prairie gardening is our rushed growing season,

Root Types

When digging your new plant into the ground, you'll quickly realize that perennial roots vary. Here are a few examples of common perennial root types.

Taproots: A taproot is a long, single primary root that penetrates deep into the ground, making plants difficult to move. A carrot is a taproot. Perennials with taproots include creeping baby's breath and globe thistle. Don't even try to divide these.

Fibrous Roots: These are the most common perennial roots and include many branching root threads that tend to be the same size and shape. Hostas have fibrous roots.

Rhizomes: Not true roots, rhizomes are actually modified stems that are horizontal and swollen. Because of this, they should not be buried deeply in the ground but covered lightly with soil. Irises grow from rhizomes.

Bulbs: Another root imposter, a bulb is a series of fleshy scales that overlap one another. To visualize what a bulb looks like, think of an onion. Lilies are perennials that spring from bulbs.

Tubers: Another type of underground fleshy stem, the most famous tuber is the potato. Day lilies are perennials with tuberous roots.

which makes spring planting the best option. The following tips will ensure easy transplantation for newly acquired spring perennials.

- ◆ First, squeeze the sides of the plastic container at its base, allowing the rooted plant to easily slide out of its encasement. Be sure to remove a thin layer of topsoil from the plant to get rid of any spores or weed seeds present.
- ◆ Next, gently shake the container upside down at a 45° angle. The roots and all will swiftly pop out. You may wish to loosen the roots if they're a tangled mess as this allows them to stretch out and quickly establish themselves in the soil.
- ◆ When preparing a spot for new perennials, make sure that a layer of compost is applied to the bottom of the hole. This will allow for drainage and will supply beneficial nutrients to the plant.
- ◆ Once the plant is positioned in the hole, fill it in with more compost and extra soil. Make sure the soil is firmly packed down around the plant's base and then water it until pooling begins.

Newly transplanted perennials should be watered every other day during the initial shock of being uprooted (for two to three weeks) and then twice weekly for the rest of the season. Keep in mind that this is merely a guide. If your plant is dry, give it a drink, and if it's soppy and turning yellow from being too wet, back off. As a rule of thumb, it takes a growing season for a perennial to establish its roots well enough for winter survival. Ensuring your perennials are well cared for will enable their continued success in your garden for years to come.

Eco-friendly Gardening

Gardening can also involve making and using your own compost and collecting rainwater, two incredibly easy ways of benefiting your plant and significantly reducing your ecological footprint on the globe. Considering the benefit to plants, the money it saves in terms of water usage and fertilizer purchases, and the benefit to the environment, there is little reason for gardeners not to go green.

Composting

Composting is an easy way of cutting down on kitchen waste and garden litter. The added bonus is that it supplies plants with superior nutrients. Although easy to do, it does take time to see results. I'll never forget seeing the most amazing compost in my friend Kim's backyard in Saskatoon. I found buckets and buckets of "black gold" in her compost bin after a bit of self-confessed backyard snooping. Overjoyed, I congratulated Kim and her husband Charles on their perfect compost production. I was really proud of them! While my friend accepted my compliments at first, she later confessed that when they first moved into their house, they didn't really use the compost bin all that much. Well, actually, they never used it. For over a year, whatever was in that black box was allowed to break down into the most perfect of soil additives without Kim or

Charles even realizing it. They had a bin full of beautiful black compost that would make any seasoned gardener envious, and their secret was that they'd left the bin alone and done nothing to it. How cool is it to be rewarded for simply doing nothing and letting nature happen?

Once you decide to begin composting your garden garbage, what do you need to begin? Most Saturday gardeners prefer a commercially made black compost box. They're easy to put together (I assembled mine myself, so anyone can do it), and aren't much of an eyesore. A second valuable item to have is a, cute, stylish pail. Stainless steel lidded varieties won't absorb odor, take up little space, and are easy to clean. When lined with cornstarch-based bags, pail collection becomes a lot less messy. While these bags don't hold liquid very well, they break down quickly when added to the compost bin and are 100 percent biodegradable.

While everything in nature eventually breaks down, there are ways to speed up the composting process if you want your black gold sooner rather than later. Once you get a compost box, the first step is to layer "green stuff" (wet matter that isn't dried out— potato peelings, for example) and "brown stuff" (crunchy dead things like old leaves)

How do you know when your compost is ready? When it develops a dirt-like look and emits an "earthy" aroma, it's good to go. The three-month-old compost above is almost ready but is still quite chunky.

in the box. While exact amounts aren't needed, a relatively even amount of green and brown stuff will give you the compost you desire. If you want compost quickly, make sure you mix it up a bit by turning over the contents of the box with your garden spade or a big fork. This ensures that all essential bacterium are spread evenly throughout the pile and that organic material will break down quickly.

There are ways to tell if more green or brown stuff is required for your heap. If your pile is soppy and smells like ammonia, add more brown stuff. If more isn't readily available, rip up some paper, cardboard, or even dryer lint (cotton and wool are natural materials) and add it to the compost. These materials are great for adding structure and soaking up moisture. If your pile is dry and nothing is happening (no heat waves come off when you poke at it), add more kitchen waste or green stuff. To speed up the process, apply a few handfuls of lawn fertilizer and your organic garbage will become dirt-like sooner.

Collecting Rainwater

We have to engage in a paradigm shift concerning water use in our country. According to the Canadian Government's Atlas of Canada Web site, Canadians, with the exception of our neighbours living south of the border, are the biggest water wasters on the planet. We feel it's our right to use as much water as possible, without regulation. In many areas of Canada, demands on the water supply are leading to municipal water rationing. Soon, this will occur in most urban and rural areas if we don't change our practices.

So what's a gardener to do? The answer is to plant wisely (the right plants for the right locations) and to develop a water collection regimen. If composting is an easy way to make a difference to the environment, collecting rainwater is a no-brainer. All that's needed is a large store-bought barrel (plastic or oak will do) or a second-hand food-grade container with a spigot. These are easily obtained through municipally sponsored eco-organizations like Calgary's own Green Calgary (http://www.greencalgary.org). While these organizations often require you to pre-order and pick up your barrels, collecting water can be as simple as setting out a forty-litre garden trug under a downspout during a prairie thunderstorm. If everyone did this every time it rained, imagine the strain that would be lifted from our water supply!

Maintenance

Perennial garden maintenance doesn't have to be labour-intensive and boring. If you take the time to ensure your perennials strongly develop early on, they'll be more resistant to diseases and won't flop over in summer winds. Plant maintenance involves watering, deadheading and pruning, thinning out, fertilizing, and staking and cleanup.

How Much Water Is Enough?

Knowing how and when to water can be tricky. Every perennial's watering needs differ. Moisture-lovers like hostas and ligularias detest dryness, while heat-lovers like cushion spurge and sedum thrive with less water. Established perennials generally

Five Reasons to Collect Rainwater

◆ Rainwater is best for plants because, unlike tap water, it contains no chlorine or alkaline.
◆ Rainwater is all natural and just the right temperature for plants.
◆ Collecting rainwater reduces runoff and limits the strain on municipal sewer systems.
◆ Rain barrels fill quickly and are easy to access.
◆ It's a ridiculously easy way of going green.

'Undulata Albomarginata' Hosta

Water-wise Gardening Resources for Prairie Residents

The following is a list of some valuable organizations and their Web sites that deal with water and environmental conservation for prairie gardeners. If your community isn't on the list, you might think about starting a green community in your area. These Web sites are full of information to get you started.

- ◆ http://www.environmentalsociety.ca
  The Saskatchewan Environmental Society (SES) Web site has great information on making your own rain barrel and on composting and water conservation. The information is particular to Saskatchewan residents but useful to all prairie dwellers.
- ◆ http://www.resourceconservation.mb.ca
  The goal of Resource Conservation Manitoba, which is based in Winnipeg, is to promote ecological sustainability through education. It has great resources for composting on the Prairies. It also advertises annual compost bin and rain barrel sales for Winnipeggers.
- ◆ http://www.gca.ca
  The Green Communities in Canada Web site offers information on naturally pesticide-free lawn care. It also offers an information kit on how you can get your own community involved in the green communities movement.
- ◆ http://www.Edmonton.ca/environmental/conservation
  The Edmonton in Bloom Web site provides a list of environmental initiatives happening in the city of Edmonton, as well as some eco-friendly gardening tips.

need less watering than recently planted ones. The reason for this is that garden newbies need to create a good strong root system that will get them through the hard times. A rule of thumb is to water your perennials once a week or, if the plants are new, twice weekly. Watering in the early morning or evening is better than in the afternoon, since water is often lost to midday evaporation. What's important is to establish a routine and avoid inconsistencies. Occasional and infrequent watering can lead to stressed-out plants that are susceptible to diseases like powdery mildew. It's not how much water plants receive, but how often they get it.

So how exactly do you water a plant? Like many Saturday gardeners, I used to think that dousing a plant's leaves was the rule. Actually, that's a major no-no. This is just a waste of the clear stuff. The best way to ensure perennials acquire adequate H_2O is to water the plant's base and surrounding soil. This practice encourages strong root development that, in turn, will enable the plant to survive better during periods of heat. While experienced gardeners may argue over the best nozzle types and watering wands ad nauseam, what is most important is to establish a consistent watering routine that ensures maximum hydration benefit to each perennial in your garden. Whether you use an old dented watering can or a high-tech sprayer is entirely up to you.

Deadheading and Pruning

One day while I was teaching a grade eight language arts class, the students and I were engaged in a discussion relating to a short story about personal growth. I stated that people, like plants, can grow and bloom after painful experiences and that perennials actually thrive once they are cut back. Then, completely off topic, one of my students shot back, "Are plants emo?" I was perplexed and had no idea what this meant. My class then (mis)informed me that the term "emo," in their lexicon, refers to a person who cuts themselves to release pain. The true definition actually refers to a teen sub-culture characterized by the wearing of skinny jeans and dark hair that flops over one's eyes, but that didn't stop my students from applying an alternate meaning of the term to my garden. While this wasn't the discussion I'd intended on having (actually, the metaphor I was shooting for flew right over their heads), I was labelled as the teacher with the "emo-garden" for the rest of the year.

While I wouldn't go so far as to say "plants are emo," it's true that most perennials benefit from being cut back after they're finished blooming. There are several reasons for this. The first is that cutting off spent blooms, or deadheading, encourages new flowers to form. The whole point of flowering for a plant is to produce seeds for repro-duction, and if dead flowers are removed, the perennial must produce new ones to achieve this purpose. Also, pruning, in general, reduces the size of the plant, which is a good thing. I have little room for out-of-control huge plants in my suburban back-yard. Pruning plants back is a must if a jungle is to be avoided. Another reason to prune involves dealing with the "3Ds," namely, damaged, diseased, and dead foliage. There's never a wrong time to prune when dealing with the 3Ds.

Deadheading doesn't only mean removing faded flower petals. Effective deadhead-ing involves removing the whole flower stem in order to prevent the plant's energy from being used up in seed production. Getting rid of the crud will make your plants look healthier and encourage new growth. Pruning should become a part of weekly garden maintenance and not a practice left just for fall or spring cleanup.

Perennials that Won't Rebloom When Cut

Not every perennial will rebloom when cut back. While blooms will only occur once a season for these plants, they still benefit from deadheading, so continue to get rid of all the spent blooms to avoid plant energy being directed toward seed production. Examples of perennials that won't rebloom when cut include:

- astilbe (*Astilbe* x *arendsii*)
- bergenia (*Bergenia cordifolia*)
- ligularia (*Ligularia* sp.)
- lily (*Lilium* hybrids)
- Siberian iris (*Iris siberica*)

Thinning out

Though hard to imagine, many perennials with multiple stems (e.g., coneflower, rudbeckia, garden phlox, beebalm) perform best when they're thinned out in the spring. This means that the weak, spindly shoots on the plant are pinched off at the base and the strong shoots are given more room to grow. When I first started gardening, I found this hard to do, as I wanted to get the most out of my perennials and thought the more plant the better. Pinched-back plants, however, perform better and appear more robust than those that are left untouched. Getting rid of the weak stems at their base will allow the healthy stems to grow stronger and look impressive. It's like applying Herbert Spencer's "survival of the fittest" to your backyard ecosystem.

Fertilizing Perennials

Saturday gardeners are always looking for a quick fix and instant impact. We want big plants with big blooms and we want them now. Many, too, are under the impression that the answer lies in generously applying store-bought synthetic fertilizers to newly purchased perennials. There are several reasons why this may not be beneficial. First, too much fertilizer can actually push plant growth too quickly and end up turning perennials into floppy green aphid magnets. Second, plants that are continually fed commercial fertilizer concoctions produce far fewer flowers than their nonjuiced counterparts. Many plants flower in response to a degree of stress and the hurried need to reproduce. If a plant is continually happy, in an addicted kind of way, there's no reason for it to reproduce, and it will produce more foliage than flowers. Third, human-made fertilizers are expensive, and the verdict is still out in terms of their long-term effects on groundwater and soil systems. While I once doused my plants with the unnatural-looking blue powdery stuff, I now find that well-rotted compost and a bag of steer manure mixed together and applied throughout the growing season are all the food my perennials need to be happy. Organics such as compost and manure enrich the soil, which may become sterile and depleted of plant nutrients as a result of consistent, long-term, synthetic fertilizer applications.

Staking and Supports

Some perennials that get big fast or have heavy blooms need extra support in maintaining their ideal posture in the garden. Stakes and plant supports provide this service. They act as "garden bras" to big floppy flowers that would otherwise droop. Different supports have different purposes. Ring supports are often used to prop up top-heavy peonies, while simple bamboo stakes and Velcro tape can secure tall hollyhocks against powerful winds. Vines definitely need support, and trellises and arches work well for this. Stakes and supports should be in place in early spring, before your plants get big. A third of the stake should be plugged into the ground so that as the plant matures, the support may be adjusted throughout the season. Knowing which perennials in your garden get big and have a tendency to fall over can help you know what kinds of stakes to buy. The following is a list of perennials that will benefit from being supported by wires or wood:

- clematis (*Clematis* sp.)
- hollyhock (*Alcea rosea*)
- honeysuckle vine (*Lonicera* x *brownii*)
- ligularia (*Ligularia* sp.)
- Asiatic lily (*Lilium* hybrids)
- Maltese cross (*Lychnis chalcedonica*)
- peachleaf bellflower (*Campanula persicifolia*)
- peony (*Paeonia lactiflora*)
- rudbeckia (*Rudbeckia fulgida* var. *sullivantii*)

When and How to Clean up the Yard

Is it a good idea to clean up in the fall and have a nice clean backyard when spring arrives, or leave the garden as is and wait until snowmelt? The best time, in my view, is to clean up the yard in the spring. There are several reasons for this. First, expired stems and stalks provide winter coverage for plants and prevent exposure to fierce prairie winters. In areas like Calgary, where perennials aren't guaranteed continual snow cover, this is essential. Second, by leaving faded plants up over the winter, you're creating four-season interest in your backyard. This means that you have something to look at in your garden when you venture out in the cold. Perennials, including coneflower and clematis, that are left in place help give structure to the garden even when most of it appears lifeless. Third, spring cleanup is invigorating and often the first step for getting out in the garden after a long winter. By fall, most of us are tired of garden work. Spring cleanup can be fun and is often done with a renewed sense of energy. Remember, not all leaves crunch up in the fall and winter, and some perennials are evergreen or semi-evergreen, much the same as pine and spruce trees. Leaving your yard cleanup until the spring can help you avoid any mistakes you may make if you happen to trash evergreen perennials in the fall.

Watching Your Plants Grow

There's nothing better than having the garden you envisioned come to life. The plants are where you want them, and favourite flowers are in continuous bloom throughout the season. But what happens in a few years when your perennials just aren't as vigorous as they used to be? Plants that are left unattended in the same spot year after year can get tired, and when they get big and don't bloom the way they used to, it's time to take action. What do you do if your perennials are out of control and are too big for your yard? If this is the case, division and container planting may be options.

The Importance of Size

As discussed earlier, it's important to have a variety of perennial sizes and shapes in the garden. Tall perennials and vines are important in adding height and "walls" to the backyard, just as ground covers act as flooring. If your multitude of perennials is becoming a jungle, you may need to change your garden plan. Most perennials do well

from being given a brush-cut after they're done flowering. This not only benefits the plant but also results in a tidier landscape. If a perennial's greenery is too big, too floppy, and has finished flowering, buzz back the plant and no harm should come of it.

Dividing Perennials

Much like people, plants can become tired and lacklustre. They may become large and out of shape and not bloom like they used to. If this is the case, your perennials need to be divided to get back into shape. You can divide your perennials early in the spring when the plants begin to emerge. If you notice that the middle of the plant appears to be dead, you need to divide it. Simply lift the whole plant from the ground with a garden spade and break off the healthy parts, composting the dead stuff. Plant the now divided healthy parts as you would a store-bought perennial, making sure it's adequately watered. Now, instead of one drab perennial, you have two or three healthy young ones that will continue to perform for you or, if you decide to share your bounty, for your friends.

Perennials in Containers

Many people assume that annuals are the only plants that can grow in containers. This is not always the case. For those gardeners with limited space in their yards, container-grown perennials are the clear choice. Once the growing season is finished, these plants must be placed back into the backyard landscape to prepare themselves for winter. Rarely do perennials survive prairie winters by remaining in exposed pots or containers. Plants in containers will quickly dry out and die if they are left to overwinter in containers. By digging out potted perennials and replanting them in the garden in the fall, you're helping the plant to stretch out its roots and (hopefully) survive the winter. Then, in the spring, the same perennial can be uprooted and repotted if need be. This is an economical way of gardening, since these perennials can be displayed in containers year after year. The following is a list of perennials that can live quite happily in containers:

- coral bells (*Heuchera* sp.)
- day lily (*Hemerocallis* sp.)
- golden creeping Jenny (*Lysimachia nummularia* 'Aurea')
- hens and chicks (*Sempervivum* sp.)
- hosta (*Hosta* sp.)
- periwinkle vine (*Vinca minor*)
- stonecrop (*Sedum* sp.)
- Siberian iris (*Iris sibirica*)
- Whitley's Veronica/speedwell (*Veronica whitleyii*)

Averting Disaster:
Dealing with Threats to Your Plants

Now for the bad news. There are threats to your plants, many of which probably haven't even been considered. Not only must you prepare to battle bugs, weeds, and diseases but unforeseen garden foes may also lurk in the cute and cuddly forms of pets and children. The following information will help ensure that your plants get off to the best start possible, and present tips in battling or dealing with garden pests that are safe and chemical-free. If you use common sense and focus on prevention, a lot can be done to keep your plants happy and relatively free from "enemy attacks."

What Is Killing My Plant?

While we may assume bugs or ourselves are to blame for plant mortality, this isn't always the case. If leaves die and plants appear ill, there may be a number of different reasons behind, or causes of, these botanical maladies. The chart below lists some common sick plant symptoms and their likely causes and how well the plant will recover, if at all.

Bugs

While we may complain about bugs on the Prairies, our short growing season and harsh climate create an unfavourable environment for many garden pests. That said, when bugs do strike, they strike hard. A first resort for many nongardeners is to reach for some kind of bug-killing spray. Many commercial pesticides, however, may be harmful to children, birds, and pets, as well as to predatory bug species. Chemical treatments including insecticidal soaps need not be the first, or only, line of defence when dealing with bugs on your plants.

If you want to have plants in your yard, bugs will follow. Not all garden bugs, however, are harmful. Many, in fact, are quite beneficial. Predators like ladybugs and garden spiders do a much better job of eliminating pest species than any human ever could. The following is a list of some (not all) of the common bugs that will probably exist in your prairie garden. At the end of the section on each bug is a verdict: to squish or not to squish. You be the judge.

Sick Plants: Symptoms, Causes, Treatment, and Prognosis

Symptoms	Probable Causes	Treatment	Prognosis
irregular hole in leaves	bugs and slugs	In the case of caterpillars and slugs, hand-picking them off the underside of leaves will work, as will hard sprays of water.	If infestations are severe, sometimes cutting off affected leaves or even the entire plant to ground level might be an option.
curled leaves	caterpillars and aphids	Pick off and squish bugs in curled leaves and then search the undersides of leaves for more pests.	If caught early, prospects for plant recovery are good.
perfectly circular hole in leaf edges	leafcutter bees	Prune off affected leaves if desired.	Bees won't do much damage to the plant, so it's best to let them do their business.
sudden appearance of gnarled, cupped, or curled leaves and stunted growth of entire plant	herbicide drift	Cut off affected parts of the plant and throw them in the garbage.	The plant may recover if cut back, or it may die entirely, depending on the amount of drift it has received.
scorched leaves	sunburn	Get your plant out of the sun. Check to see if your plant is a shade-lover. If it is, move it.	Plants that get too much sun can recover if they are moved early in the season. Remember to plant like plants in like conditions.
broken stems and leaves	kids, pets, or hail	Cover unprotected plants with old, light sheets when hailstorms are suspect and avoid planting tender plants in play areas.	Cutting back broken parts of the plant may help. If the entire plant has been squashed, cut it near to the ground and it may come back.
spots, rust, or ugly fuzzy appearance	diseases	Cut back affected areas and then disinfect your gardening tools.	Plants can often recover from diseases when affected areas are cut out. See the table on common plant diseases later in this chapter.

continued on next page

Symptoms	Probable Causes	Treatment	Prognosis
yellow leaves	possible mineral deficiency, overwatering, or insufficient sunlight	Make sure all plants receive the right amount of water in a consistent manner. Extremely alkaline soils can be corrected by adding chelated iron. Test the soil and then seek professional help.	While yellow leaves can be pruned off, yellow plants that should be green are sick plants. It might be best to compost them and start over.
lifeless leaves and stems that appear at first mushy and then dry to a crisp	frost	Make sure all of your perennials that are listed above zone 3 get adequate protection when the temperature falls below freezing.	While many perennials recover from light frost damage, most won't survive prolonged periods of frost. Don't worry, they will emerge again in the spring.
light-coloured squiggle lines appear on leaves	leaf miner bugs	Remove and compost individual leaves as they appear.	Generally, leaf miners aren't a huge problem and appear sporadically, rather than en masse. They seldom harm entire plants.

Aphids

Most everyone has experienced the scourge of aphids. They swarm over plants in the late summer, and drop sticky "honeydew" (aphid poop) on cars parked under trees in the fall. Aphid attacks are all too common on the Prairies. Aphids are a formidable foe in the garden, but before you reach for the bug spray, there are a few things that you need to know.

Aphids are tiny, squishy, tear-drop-shaped insects that suck the sap out of plants. Their colouring includes varying shades of green, black, red, and tan, and they rarely exceed 2 mm in length. There are more than 1,300 aphid species in North America. A small suburban garden may be filled with loads of diverse aphid types at any given time. Aphids are also plant-specific and one species alone won't invade every plant in a garden space. Aphids on your phlox will usually not be the same ones that go after your hostas.

Aphid reproduction is, to say the least, unbelievable. Normally, aphids reproduce asexually. Females that hatch in the spring will give birth to live female babies without any male assistance. These babies, in turn, are born pregnant! This ensures that several generations are produced in a single season. Sexual reproduction does occur but only among one generation per year. Winged males fly to host plants to mate with special females, who in turn lay eggs that overwinter on the undersides of leaves. The whole crazy cycle then begins again the following spring.

The cycle of the aphid is bizarre, to say the least, but it does explain the sheer numbers of them that thrive in our gardens. Knowing what you're up against is key in battling the aphid armies. They do severely outnumber us, but hope is not lost. It's worth noting that if you have a plant being ravaged by aphids, it was probably stressed before the masses came. Aphids seldom destroy healthy, thriving specimens. So, if you have plants that are persistently overrun by aphid herds, they were probably unhappy before the leaf-suckers struck.

Verdict: Squish and squish some more.

The Aphid/Ant Relationship

If you've ever noticed ants scrambling along plants infested with aphids, you've witnessed a very bizarre symbiotic relationship. Though people often think many species of ants eat aphids, they don't. Simply put, they milk them! Ants love honeydew. In order to acquire it, they herd aphids (much as a shepherd herds sheep) around so that the small green bugs are able to feed on plants. The ants are then rewarded with honeydew from aphid-stroking. In exchange for the honeydew, the ants offer the aphids protection. It's a weird partnership but it works for both the ranching ants and their aphid herds.

Dealing with an Aphid Invasion

◆ If you have an aphid infestation, check to see whether or not your plant is in the right location and if it has received proper care. Aphids are attracted to plants that are stressed-out.

◆ Aphids are easily dislodged from plants with a hard spray of water from a hose. They usually won't make it back to the host plant once they've been forcefully sprayed off. You may have to hold a bloom with one hand while you guide the hose nozzle with the other in order to knock off the little suckers.

◆ A large concentration of aphids on affected plants usually means that predators like ladybugs are hard at work stuffing themselves on an aphid buffet. The use of insecticides—which seldom work once you notice the aphid hordes—also kills beneficial insects like ladybugs and lacewings. Let the predators do their job.

Slugs

The grossest of the gross, slugs and snails aren't actually insects but animals known as gastropods and are the cousins of mollusks and clams. Unlike insects, their bodies aren't segmented. They're four centimetres of squishiness covered in slime. While we don't have terrestrial snails in our prairie gardens, slugs are another story.

Slugs inflict significant damage on young, tender plants and new growth. They're particularly fond of hostas, leaving smoothly edged holes behind as evidence of their existence. Slugs thrive in moist, humid conditions and render their destruction when the sun goes down or is behind cover. You will seldom see slugs during the day, as they detest sun, heat, and dry conditions. During daylight hours, they hide under rocks, mulch, flowerpots, or any other form of garden cover. The key to battling slugs is in knowing the enemy.

Sexing Slugs

Slugs are hermaphrodites, meaning they have both male and female parts. However, slugs often go through periods when they are distinctly male or female. They may change their sex, depending on the circumstances they're faced with. For example, in order to produce eggs, a slug must mate with another. If there are too many mostly "female" slugs around, some individuals will inevitably turn into "males" in order for reproduction to occur.

Since slugs love to hide, eliminating such enticing spots in your garden is important. In areas that are frequently watered, get rid of rocks, wooden boards, mulch layers, or anything that could become a slug safe house. Pulling back layers of mulch from the base of plants is also important. I've found that methods such as scattering eggshells and nonchemical store-bought remedies are largely ineffective in battling slugs.

There are two things that work best in the defence against these "slimers." The first is the use of copper netting. Placed 9-cm-deep around specific plants, the copper mesh is an effective slug repellent. The copper is said to react with the slug's slime, causing a chemical reaction and zapping it with electricity. Copper pot scrubbers sold cheaply at department stores work well as slug deterrents. While it may be impractical to use copper throughout the garden, for feature plants this may be a useful method.

The second effective method of slug elimination is (gulp) hand-picking. Yes, it's ugly, but if you put on gloves, it's not too bad (who am I kidding; yes, it is). If you have small children, they may even be fooled into thinking slug-picking is a game of sorts (the one with the most slime wins!). Hand-picking is best done after sundown, with a flashlight, or in the early morning when the slugs are out in full force. Remember not to do this while wearing lacy pajamas, as the neighbours will think you're nuts.

Finally, if you really hate slugs, create a dry rock garden with drought-loving plants. Slugs hate the heat. They also detest gliding across fine sharp-edged rocks and will shrivel up in such conditions. Having instituted this design in one area of my garden, I'm happy to say that it works quite well.

Verdict: Squish with vigour.

Yellow Jackets and Wasps

Who doesn't shiver when they meet up with a wasp? These stingers can cause fear in the bravest of souls. It's with good reason we dread them, too. They're the pit bulls of the insect world, known to decapitate their victims midflight with unmatched viciousness. Flailing your arms in fright will only make them meaner, so don't do it. Like approaching a bully on the playground, your best bet is to avoid eye contact and act in an inconspicuous manner. That said, both wasps and yellow jackets are fierce predators of garden pests.

Verdict: Don't swat at or squish them. They do their job, and will hurt you when angered.

Ladybugs

In spite of their sweet name, ladybugs are among the garden's most ravenous predators. Their choice of prey being aphids makes them a welcome sight in any garden. These predators attack and consume aphids with a primordial ferocity that makes one question the cuteness we attribute to them. One single ladybug can consume several hundred aphids in a given day. Nearly two hundred species of ladybug inhabit North America, a few of them originally introduced from overseas. The ladybug larva is very different in appearance from the adult version. Junior ladybugs have an alligator-like appearance and look nothing like mom or dad. They also eat many more aphids than their seniors during their growth spurts.

Verdict: Don't squish anything that resembles a vicious reptile, as it's probably a beneficial predator.

Ladybug Facts

◆ Adult ladybugs spend the winter in sheltered locations throughout the garden, including under leaf piles and scattered compost. In spring, try not to disturb these areas until after the bugs are awake, around late March.
◆ The old adage that a ladybug's age can be determined by the number of spots on its wings is simply untrue. A ladybug's spots are determined by its species and don't increase with age.
◆ During the Middle Ages, this bug was dedicated as the "Beetle of the Lady" (Virgin Mary), hence the name "ladybug."
◆ Ladybugs are viewed as forerunners of good luck and nice weather in many parts of Europe.

Spiders

Like many, I hate spiders. Though they creep me out, I do like having them in my garden. Spiders are truly amazing predators that see the world as a dichotomy between things that can be eaten—including other spiders—and things that cannot—like rocks. Being a bit of a self-described sadist, I'd enjoy seeing spiders suck the juices out of ensnared aphids, if I wasn't so scared of them. That said, I've often placed my young daughter on web patrol in order to free ladybugs and damselflies that have flown into possible peril. Despite the major yuck-factor, spiders have a huge role to play in keeping pest populations in check.

Verdict: In spite of their gross appearance and questionable culinary tastes, don't squish.

Daddy Longlegs

Distant cousins of spiders, more than two hundred species of daddies exist throughout North America. Some of these insects were introduced from Europe. Like spiders, daddies have eight legs, but unlike their cousins, they lack poison glands and don't spin webs. Daddy longlegs are varied in their eating habits and consume everything from slugs and dead spiders, to plant juice.

Verdict: Despite their varied palates, daddies are effective predators and shouldn't be squished.

Sci-Fi Spiders

The common garden spider injects a poison into its victims that acts quickly to liquefy their insides. Afterward, the spider will suck out the bug like a slushie drink and leave the carcass behind as garbage. It almost sounds like something from a bad 1950s sci-fi movie, but it happens right in your backyard.

Sowbugs

These bugs resemble prehistoric trilobites and aren't actually insects. Belonging to the class Crustacea, they're related to lobsters and shrimp. Originally from Europe, sowbugs are scavengers that feed on decaying plant material. They do little damage to healthy plant material, and tend to be nocturnal, venturing out only on overcast days. Considering that they don't harm plants and have an intriguing prehistoric look, I don't mind them in my garden at all.

Verdict: Don't squish; it's like having a part of prehistory in your backyard.

Ground Beetles

These big black beetles look mean and live up to their appearance. Fairly common in the garden, ground beetles do a decent job of eliminating ground-level pests. Ground beetles are carnivores and don't harm plant material. They're often found underneath big rocks and garden structures.

Verdict: Resist any desire to hear the crunch of the beetle's exoskeleton. In other words, don't squish.

Damselflies and Dragonflies

These bombers are by far the coolest garden insects. Not only are dragons and damsels the fastest bugs in the garden but they're effective predators as well, often snatching their prey midflight. Damselflies are slighter in appearance than dragonflies, and unlike their cousins, can position their wings vertically along their bodies or spread them at a slight angle (the "spreadwings"). Damselflies also have clearly separated eyes, while the dragonfly's eyes are so close together they almost look attached.

Verdict: Don't squish them; they're neat to watch as they zip around.

Weeds

A weed is any unwanted plant that exists in your garden space. If you like dandelions growing in your yard, and use their young shoots in spring salads, they're not weeds. If you detest the space they take up, like I do, then they're weeds. The definition of "weed" is a matter of perception and opinion.

Prairie dragonflies are often quite large and are characterized by huge nearly joined eyes and vertically positioned wings.

Neighbourly Advice

Jeff deJong, my master gardener instructor in Calgary, gave me some sound advice. He said if your neighbour offers you a plant that was growing in their garden, kindly accept it but promptly trash it behind closed doors. Why? It may be an invasive weed like creeping bellflower. If your neighbour doesn't want the plant, why should you?

Typically, weeds are invasive plants that seek to take over your garden with a military-like ambition. The goal of every weed is to out-compete your garden babies for space, light, water, and nutrients. Perennials that are crowded out by weeds will remain small, and won't produce flowers like they should. Weeds must be destroyed, or at the very least controlled, in the garden.

As a first line of defence, many Saturday gardeners are tempted to reach for chemicals as a solution to problematic weeds. There are, however, other methods of addressing these garden nasties. Since urbanites are dealing with weeds on a smaller scale, these methods don't use up a lot of time. To rural residents and acreage owners, I can only say good luck and that I feel sorry for you in regard to weed infestations (having grown up on a farm, I know your plight). The following is a list of tips and treatments to use in battling unwanted weeds that don't involve chemical control.

- The best time to weed is after it rains, when weeds like dandelions are easily pulled from the ground.
- Don't allow weeds to flower and go to seed or you'll be battling their children all summer long. Simply snapping off a flower head is an easy way of limiting the number of potential weeds in your garden.
- Avoid buying so-called wild flower mixes and planting them. Invasive plants, including creeping bellflower, might be included in this hodgepodge.

The good thing about living on the Prairies is that our short growing season doesn't allow for an extended season of weeds. The types that thrive here, however, have adapted very well to the prairie climate. The following table lists the weeds and invasive plants common to the Canadian Prairies.

Mulch and Landscape Fabric

The word "mulch" is a broad term. It refers to anything that's used to top-dress the soil in garden beds or around plants. Mulch can include bark chips, rocks, cocoa shells, or even grass clippings. Mulch has a number of purposes in the garden. First, it acts as a barrier against emerging weeds and helps prevent them from taking up valuable space.

Common Prairie Weeds

Common Weeds and Invasive Plants	Flower Features	ID Features
Canada Thistle (*Cirsium arvense*)	purple blooms from July to October	Seriously thorny prickles exist along the edge of the stems on this plant.
Creeping Bellflower (*Campanula rapunculoides*)	purple-blue blooms from June to August; produces up to three thousand seeds in a growing season	This plant has heart-shaped leaves that become more slender further up the stalk. It has a pretty flower, but avoid keeping this one in your garden at all costs.
Field Bindweed (*Convolvulus arvensis*)	white morning-glory-like flowers	This plant has arrow-shaped leaves that climb along fences or form mats. Even though they look pretty, pull out anything that looks like a vine that you know you didn't plant.
Dandelion (*Taraxacum officinale*)	yellow pompoms that quickly turn into fluffy seed heads; blooms are an important source of pollen for many bee species	This plant has jagged-edged leaves that were traditionally used in salads across Europe. Dandelions were introduced to North America because of their popularity in Europe.
Common Chickweed (*Stellaria media*)	tiny star-shaped white blooms	This plant has small leaves that are oval with pointed ends. Each plant can produce over fifteen thousand seeds per season. With the possibility of four generations of plants per season, that's over fifteen million seeds!

Origin	Size and Type	Control Methods
Southeastern Eurasia	1.5-m-tall perennial weed	Control this plant by hand-pulling it using protective gloves.
Europe	1-m-tall creeping perennial that chokes out other plants	Digging out the whole plant ensures the weed won't come back from its rhizomes. Don't compost it, as it will continue to survive on the pile. Throw it in the garbage ASAP. Once established, it's hard to get rid of.
Eurasia	1-m-tall twining perennial that will quickly choke out other garden dwellers	Hand-pulling and hoeing will help reduce seed production. Seeds can be viable for up to thirty years. Broken-off roots can replant themselves and quickly take off, so be careful.
Eurasia (traditionally used for medicinal purposes)	30-45-cm-tall perennial weed	Hand-digging dandelions with a specialized weed digger works, as does pouring boiling water directly onto the plant before removing it. Be sure to get the taproot removed or the plant will come back. This is best done when the plant is wet.
Europe (traditionally used to feed livestock and soothe irritated skin)	low-growing mat-forming perennial	Common chickweeds can be hand-pulled and hoed before seeds are set. They can also be mowed down.

Second, it helps prevent evaporation and cuts down on the amount of watering needed. It also protects plants from severe winter cold and prairie summer heat by acting as an insulator. Finally, certain types of mulch, like bark chips and rocks, can add a decorative element to your garden space. Usually, a 5-cm depth of mulch is all that's needed. Appling a layer of mulch to your plants is definitely worth the effort.

Before adding mulch, a base layer of landscape fabric should be used. Landscape fabric is often made out of black mesh, with a light, felt-like texture. Usually anchored down with pegs, it can be easily snipped to adjust to any size. While it may be applied to existing beds, this is often a difficult process and something that should be attempted only if you have relatives coming to visit ("Hey bro, it's good to have you stay for the weekend . . . Now, about that favour you owe me . . . "). Once you lay it down, you must cut holes into the fabric to create space for your desired perennials. Once the landscape fabric is in place, unwanted plants aren't given a chance to grow. The application of mulch and landscape fabric is an effective method of weed prevention and will save on weed-pulling backaches down the road.

Plant Diseases

When plants wilt and look sick, we tend to blame ourselves for not supplying them with enough water, but very often we're not directly to blame. Oftentimes, soil-borne diseases like viruses, fungi, and bacteria are the root cause (pardon the bad pun), and can exist in the garden for decades. There are steps Saturday gardeners can take to prevent plant diseases. First, it's important to buy hardy varieties of perennials. Many of the top choices listed in Chapter 6 are disease-resistant, and this information is usually listed on the plant tags. Second, you must remember to regularly and consistently water your new perennials. As mentioned earlier, it's not how much water plants receive but how often they get it that makes them happy.

If you have to dig out or deal with diseased plants, always wash off your tools and gloves in soapy water so as not to transfer disease to the rest of your garden plants. It's also wise not to compost any diseased plant parts, as viruses, bacteria, and fungi can exist dormant in soil for up to twenty years. If you spend a lot of time battling disease in a particular plant, the best bet may be to junk it and start over with a different perennial choice or a resistant cultivar.

So how do you spot plant diseases? The following table lists some common perennial diseases, their symptoms, steps to take in treatment, and the plants that are commonly affected.

Pets, Kids, and Gardening

We tend to associate garden disasters with bugs or weeds. In my yard, however, more plants have been injured due to soccer games and dogs than by slugs or aphids. What happens when kids, pets, and perennials all seek coexistence in the same space? While it may seem like a lot of work, there are simple ways to ensure that everyone is happy and the plants don't end up being trashed.

Common Plant Diseases

Disease	Symptoms	Treatment	Affected Plants
Botrytis Blight	shoots wilt and droop, turning black; leaf buds turn black and die	Get rid of sickly parts of the plant; make sure plants are in a well-drained site.	peonies, lilies
Bacterial Leaf Spot	many small brown or purple spots develop, and leaves turn yellow	Throw out infected plants (don't compost). Wash your hands and tools!	poppies, cranesbills
Fungal Leaf Spot	leaves develop brown, black, or yellow spots and wither	Get rid of infected leaves. Make sure your plants aren't crowded to ensure maximum possible air circulation.	many different perennials
Powdery Mildew	grey or white fungal patches appear on the upper surfaces of leaves; may affect the entire plant and cause distortion like leaf-curling	Remove and throw out the infected parts of the plant. Make sure your plants get good air circulation early on in the season.	coneflowers, rudbeckias, beebalms, phloxes
Rust	fungus that covers the undersides of leaves with tiny powdery spots that are orange or yellow; causes leaves to wilt and drop	Remove and throw the infected leaves in the garbage. Also, avoid allowing your plants to stand in pools of water.	hollyhocks, bellflowers, beebalms, clematises, irises, blazing stars
Viruses	leaves appear yellow and mottled, or streaked; plants often puny	There's no cure for viruses. Throw the plant in the garbage, clean your tools, and start over. Viruses are spread via insects like aphids.	peonies, lilies, irises, blanket flowers

Pets

People often think if they have pets, gardening will be impossible. Dogs can dig up plants in a matter of minutes, while wandering cats may be tempted to use well-manicured beds as litter boxes. It's possible to have both pets and plants together in the same backyard space. All that's needed is a bit of planning and recognition of the task at hand.

As far as unleashed cats are concerned, people worry needlessly. My mother would always complain about the neighbourhood cats running through her backyard. Her biggest fear was that her perennial borders might be used as a litter box. This was until my grandma reminded her that cats do a lot to keep the mouse population in check. Mice are everywhere, and no one likes the idea of them running amok in our backyards. Cats are cuddly and sweet, but they're also efficient predators. While no one in an urban area likes to see cats roaming the neighbourhood, they instinctually do their job. If this still doesn't deter you from chasing away local felines, bury some chicken wire in and around your garden beds. Cats hate digging their claws into metal and this method seems to work quite well.

Though cats are usually happily kept indoors, having a dog may pose more of a problem when establishing a garden. First, a few things need to be realized by the dog owner. No individual canine breed is perfect. My German Shepherd Jessie has a huge desire to please, and a real sense of right and wrong behaviour. In front of me, she plays the role of the garden guardian; no birds or squirrels dare enter when Jessie is on patrol! She would never enter a planted area, either. When my back is turned, however, Jessie becomes Jekyll and Hyde; she enters my beds, digs, and for some strange reason, loves to destroy my 'Karl Foerster' feather reed ornamental grass. No matter how amazing your pet is, if you have one and plan on planting, you need to take steps to prevent disaster.

Dogs dig; it's part of who they are. Because of this, our canine friends must be shown where soil excavation is acceptable, and where it's not. If you have a dog, set aside a specific digging spot in your yard just for them. Place toys and treats in this area to make it a preferred spot. I have a huge sandbox where both my dog and kids are allowed to dig. I also try to make my beds less appealing to my dog. Jessie hates digging through rocks and landscape fabric, so most of my beds are covered with these materials. I've observed that she loves digging in bark mulch, and so I've eliminated this ground covering from my yard. Watch and learn from your dog's behaviour. Terriers are tenacious diggers and might rip through landscape fabric in short order. Labrador retrievers are big dogs that like to roughhouse, so try to avoid developing garden beds in their prime play areas. Knowing how your dog acts in your yard and anticipating their behaviour can prevent your backyard from looking like a war zone.

Another dilemma pet owners face is what to do when their dogs "go" in the garden. It may sound simplistic, but this is best avoided by showing them where it's acceptable to defecate and where it isn't. You can create dog runs away from the main garden, where your pooch can poop in peace. Every time your dog has used the right spot, give them a treat and lots of praise. Take them to the chosen area every time you let them out to go to the bathroom, instead of opening up the patio door for them to roam the backyard. If you don't follow through with this throughout the winter, your yard will be a soup of fecal matter when spring arrives. Dogs don't like to have a messy play area, and if you make gardening an enjoyable experience for them (second-hand experience, of course!), they're less apt to use your beds as a toilet. When I weed my beds with Jessie, I often bring along a Frisbee for a few throws. My dog actually enjoys gardening with me—every time I put on my gloves, she picks up her throw toy and jumps from side to side in excited anticipation. If gardening becomes fun for your dog, everyone and everything will benefit, especially your plants.

Kids

Kids may pose another challenge when establishing a garden. It's not the digging that's problematic (unless, of course, Tonka trucks are a factor) but play in general. My kids have little consideration for my plants when engaged in a serious game of tag or back-yard soccer. In fact, accent plants occasionally become goal posts at my house! I've learned not to place beds between the back door of the house and the kids' play area. Perennials will be trampled, and garden ornaments will fly if they get in the way of play. Plants with tender leaves, such as hostas, should be placed out of the paths of active youngsters.

Kids love helping out in the garden. As with dogs, if you make the garden an invit-ing place, children will be less apt to destroy it if they see it as their own. A recent trend in many urban landscapes is toward children's gardens. These include planted peren-nials that appeal to the senses (plants that have bold flowers, fuzzy leaves, and pleasant scents), and stand up to a child's intrusion. Though parents always fear the possibility of children eating toxic plants, most harmful perennials taste really bad, which dis-courages any kind of excessive sampling. Even so, young children should never be left unattended in the garden. The list below includes perennials that are a good choice for a children's garden.

Perennials Kids Love

- blue fescue ornamental grass (*Festuca glauca*)—appealing texture and shape, good to run hands through
- coneflower (*Echinacea purpurea*) and rudbeckia (*Rudbeckia fulgida* var. *sullivantii*)—soft daisy-like petals, hard centres, and bright colours
- hens and chicks (*Sempervivum* spp.)—appealing texture and shape
- lamb's ear (*Stachys byzantina*)—fuzzy to the touch
- pinks (*Dianthus* spp.)—great clove-like scent and vivid colours
- thrift (*Armeria maritima*)—lollypop-like flowers are great for picking
- woolly thyme (*Thymus psuedolanuginosis*)—fuzzy texture and strong scent

CHAPTER SIX

Fifty Great Perennials for the Prairies

Now that you have a clearer idea of what you want your yard to become, it's time to start choosing plants. The following is a list of fifty perennials that thrive in prairie gardens. Most of the photos in this chapter were taken in my own garden or those of close friends, so I know from first- or second-hand experience that these plants thrive on the Prairies. Each is given an explanation and description in terms of growing conditions, along with tips on obtaining peak performance.

The "Quick Notes" in this chapter offer a handy reference when purchasing or planting perennials—they describe the colour, shape, size, preferred location, and pros and cons of the listed plant. The "Top Choice Varieties" headings offer varieties of plants to try that differ a bit from the regular plant species described but are worth a glance. In addition, information is given on the history and origin of each plant. Perennials are listed alphabetically, by common name, with their botanical names listed directly below. While all of the plants listed are reliable and relatively easy to grow, remember to grow what you like, and like what you grow. Have fun!

Perennial Types in this Book

Different perennials fill diverse roles in the garden. Big, medium, and small perennials all have a part to play and work together in the creation of any ideal garden. Below is a description of the perennial types listed in this book.

Ground Covers: Short and low to the ground, they often form mats with defined borders. They act as garden rugs, protecting taller perennials from exposure and preventing water evaporation. Many, like thyme and maiden pinks, don't mind a small amount of foot traffic. Ground covers can be placed at the front of the garden or planted to cascade over the edge of a raised bed.

Edgers: These are mid-sized perennials that fill in the spots where borders would look too big and ground covers would go unnoticed. Edgers may be used to fill in areas that look bare, or supply texture and foliage along the garden's rim.

Borders: These are the first perennials to be noticed in a garden. With these plants the phrase, "go big or go home" is applicable. While a small garden full of border plants may be too overpowering, a simple mixture will add height and substance to a landscape.

Vines: These climbers add a ceiling to the garden as they grow up and over fences or arbours and help to tie in houses and other structures with the landscape.

Ornamental Grasses: These grasses should be allowed to grow to their full potential and not be mowed. They're treated as regular perennials and grown for their texture and foliage.

Jackmanii Clematis

Artemisia/Wormwood
Artemisia stelleriana, A. schmidtiana

I really enjoy the silvery contrast these perennials provide when paired up with flowering plants. The value of artemisia is in the superior foliar effect it creates. Since these plants aren't grown for their blooms, I cut back the tiny ugly flowers once they appear in summer. Doing this creates a plant with a super silvery look that makes nearby blossoms pop out at passersby. It looks great individually in the front of a bed, or planted close to bold flowers such as coneflowers. 'Silver Brocade' (*A. stelleriana*) looks like the annual commonly called dusty miller, and only one plant is needed to cover a small area. It looks grand planted by grasses or spiky types of perennials like blazing star. Artemisia is a great choice for the prairie garden, as it's very easy to grow, and once established it tolerates neglect. There are many types of artemisia that do well in prairie gardens, but 'Silver Brocade' and its cousin 'Silver Mound' (*A. schmidtiana*) (this plant looks like the fibre-optic-type lights that teens adorn their bedrooms with) are my favourites. Not a lot of water or attention is needed during the summer for artemisia to shine. Dig it in as an accent plant beside other summertime heat-lovers and you won't be let down.

QUICK NOTES

Perennial Type: Semi-evergreen edger or ground cover.

Top Choice Varieties: 'Silver Mound' (clumping edger); 'Silver Brocade' (creeping ground cover).

Flower Colour and Type: Irrelevant, since these plants are used for their foliage.

Foliage Colour and Texture: Varying shades of silver; fine fern-like texture.

Size: Medium—15-20 cm tall and 30-40 cm across.

Site Location: The more sun the better for these drought-lovers. Once established, they need little water. Artemisia are best placed in front of larger plants. Place at the front of the flowerbed as an accent plant and it will quickly fill in an area.

Perfect Partners: In front of coneflower, blazing star, rudbeckia, or clematis.

Name/Origin/History: Named after the Greek goddess of the hunt, Artemis, this plant was popularly used in Roman times. Artemisia plants native to Greece were in bloom when hunters returned to the woods after winter, and this is one possible source of the name. The word "stelleriana" is associated with German Georg Steller (1709-1746), a plant collector. It originates from Europe and Northwest Asia.

Pros: Artemisia is related to native prairie sagebrush (not culinary sage) and has a pungent scent that deters many pests.

Cons: It needs to be divided every year or two in order to look its best.

Tips: Shear off the flowers and excess foliage in mid to late summer if it becomes too floppy.

Throughout the centuries, artemisia has been valued for killing parasitic worms, hence its other common name, wormwood ('Silver Brocade' pictured here).

The spring foliage of some astilbes ('Fanal' pictured here)
is a bronze colour that turns a deep green in the summer.

Astilbe

Astilbe x arendsii, A. simplicifolia

While few shade-lovers offer vibrant blooms, astilbe is the exception. Producing flowers with the texture of a feather duster, these perennials add oomph when placed near larger-leaved plants including hosta, coral bells, and ligularia. While there are many types of astilbe available, the two listed above are great prairie performers that are hardy and don't take up a lot of room. The thing to remember with astilbes is that if they dry out they go drab immediately. However, with the right soil (rich and organic with lots of compost added throughout the season) and mulch on top to conserve moisture, these plants don't need much attention. You'll know your astilbe is unhappy if its leaves turn brown and curly. This is one of the few plants listed in this chapter that will not benefit from deadheading—I leave faded blooms in place once they've dried. If you're careful about placing this perennial, you won't be disappointed, as its unique flowers look great in the shade.

QUICK NOTES

Perennial Type: Herbaceous border.

Top Choice Varieties: 'Fanal' (red); 'Sprite' (pale pink).

Flower Colour and Type: Plume-like blooms in red, pink, lavender, and white.

Foliage Colour and Texture: Fine feathery foliage in green and bronze-green.

Size: Medium to large—30-60 cm tall and 25-60 cm across (check tags as sizes vary).

Site Location: Astilbes love moist, shady spots. A small degree of morning sun is ideal for their growth, and rich organic soil that's continually moist will ensure happy plants.

Perfect Partners: Near hosta, bleeding heart, and coral bells.

Name/Origin/History: Originating from the woodlands of China and Japan. Ironically, the word *astilbe* is Greek for "not brilliant" and refers to a few select dull-leaved species. *Arendsii* is the namesake of German plant guy Georg Arends (1863-1952) and *simplicifolia* means "simple leaves."

Pros: This plant provides bright colour for shaded gardens.

Cons: Astilbes quickly fade in dry conditions.

Tips: Astilbes need to be divided every two to three years to remain happy and healthy.

Avens, Boris

Geum coccineum 'Borisii'

Offering a neat tidy mound of geranium-like leaves, avens offer one of the the brightest orange colours around. The flowers are small and star-shaped, and though bright, aren't gaudy in the least. The orange looks great against a backdrop of green fuzzy leaves or planted near purple or indigo blooms. The colour of these perennials is unparalleled in the garden, and for those who adore flashy hues, it's a must. Flowering begins in midsummer and continues on into late August. While avens may not be long-lived in the garden, the 'Boris' variety takes well to division every two to three years. This will encourage plants to remain vigorous and keep a compact size. Avens are a reliably hardy mid-sized perennial with palm-sized, fuzzy jagged leaves that present a great backdrop to its rockin' blooms.

QUICK NOTES

Perennial Type: Evergreen or semi-evergreen clumping edger.

Flower Colour and Type: Scarlet-orange star-shaped flowers on long wiry stems above the leaves.

Foliage Colour and Texture: Fuzzy kidney-shaped leaves; midgreen in colour.

Size: Medium—30-50 cm tall and 30 cm across.

Site Location: These plants can be placed near the front of a border in full to part sun. Avens like organic soil and consistent watering during the first year in order to establish strong roots.

Perfect Partners: In front of peachleaf bellflower, rudbeckia; near catmint.

Name/Origin/History: Native to the Balkans through to Turkey, the Latin name *geum* has been used since Roman times and is derived from the Greek *geno*, referring to the clove-like aroma of the plant's roots, while *coccineum* means "scarlet." The meaning of "avens" is obscure but has been used since the Middle Ages. Though it's unclear who "Boris" was, it's evident he liked orange.

Pros: Avens require low maintenance, and they supply an extended period of spring colour.

Cons: Avens may experience dieback if exposed during the winter, so mulch is required.

Tips: Deadhead regularly to ensure continuous flowering.

Avens were used in amulets in ancient times
to ward off evil spirits and poisonous creatures.

An added bonus of baby's breath ('Rosea' pictured here) is its mild, clean fragrance, which is said to resemble that of an infant.

Baby's Breath, Creeping
Gypsophila repens

Baby's breath isn't only the staple of the flower arranging business—it also works as an effective ground cover. Anyone who has travelled near a prairie cemetery could easily sneer at the aggressive nature of baby's breath. It seems to be everywhere! Creeping baby's breath is different. Though it does spread easily by seed, this baby's breath won't take over your garden. It does extremely well in raised beds and resembles fog as it skirts over any edge. The flowers are tiny, no bigger than the nail of a pinkie finger. The plant blooms in early summer and lasts a month. This perennial is very tolerant of heat and actually prefers the alkalinity of prairie soils. While baby's breath may appear tender, it's tough and makes a habit of firmly entrenching its roots when dug in. This makes transplanting it difficult, as this is one plant that won't take to being moved easily. Baby's breath loves hot, dry areas in which many other perennials would shrivel.

QUICK NOTES

Perennial Type: Semi-evergreen ground cover.

Top Choice Varieties: 'Alba' (white); 'Rosea' (light pink).

Flower Colour and Type: White or pink panicles.

Foliage Colour and Texture: Grey-green, with tiny strip-like leaves.

Size: Small—15-20 cm tall and 30-40 cm across.

Site Location: Plant baby's breath in full sun in hot, dry locations. It does well in raised beds spilling over the edge.

Perfect Partners: In front of day lily and coneflower.

Name/Origin/History: Native to northwestern Spain, the Latin *gypso* means "chalk" and *philos* means "loving," referring to this plant's preference for alkaline soil, while *repens* means "creeping."

Pros: Creeping baby's breath doesn't need much attention or water throughout the summer.

Cons: It can suffer winter dieback if its soil is soppy. Some of its cultivars are short-lived.

Tips: Make sure this ground cover is placed in well-drained soil where it will thrive. Dividing and moving this plant is nearly impossible due to the long taproots it forms, so assume it cannot be uprooted when you first plant it. Place it near spring bulbs that go dormant in the summer to hide yellow foliage.

Beebalm
Monarda hybrids

Beebalm makes passersby take notice. This perennial offers unique blooms resembling a crazy hairstyle. In addition, it's a very aromatic plant. One of its alternate titles is Oswego tea, a name given by early Europeans to the concoctions introduced to them by the Oswego First Nations of New York state. The mild tea made from the plant's leaves is quite enjoyable, but if more than one cup is required for drinking, your plant can become defoliated quickly. Traditionally, the oil from this plant was used by shamanic healers and is still harvested for use in naturopathic medicine. Beebalm also goes by the name "bergamot," which refers to the plant's aroma, said to resemble that of the bergamot orange (no relation). Beebalm, as the name suggests, is attractive to insects like butterflies and bees. The one problem plaguing beebalm is its susceptibility to the dreaded powdery mildew, but this can be avoided by planting newer tougher varieties. Ideal conditions for this fuzzy-headed flower are moist organic soil, in part to full sun. The more compost it gets, the better. This perennial is so unique that one small clump will attract attention.

QUICK NOTES

Perennial Type: Herbaceous border.

Top Choice Varieties: 'Marshall's Delight' (rose pink), 'Coral Reef' (deep pink), 'Cambridge Scarlet' (bright red).

Flower Colour and Type: Pink, purple, red, or white blooms that look like a dreadlocked hairdo.

Foliage Colour and Texture: Dark green mint-shaped leaves.

Size: Medium to large—45-90 cm tall and 30-60 cm across (check tags as sizes vary).

Site Location: Plant beebalm in full to part sun in moist, rich soil near the back of a border.

Perfect Partners: Near coneflower and blazing star.

Name/Origin/History: Beebalm is a North American native. Its botanical name comes from Nicholas Monardes (1493-1588), a Spanish physician and botanist who was the first person to create a listing of medicinal plants of North America.

Pros: Beebalm has a great aroma and unique blooms.

Cons: It's prone to powdery mildew and aphid attacks.

Tips: Plant beebalm in a breezy location to prevent the dreaded mildew, however, modern beebalm plants are more resistant to this disease.

Beebalm ('Coral Reef' pictured here) was used by many First Nations shamans in traditional medicine. It's a member of the mint family.

*In their natural setting, these blue beauties grow along
wooded edges and in the meadows of the European Balkans.*

Bellflower, Peachleaf
Campanula persicifolia

While the word "bellflower" may bring to mind images of invasive plants, this perennial is in a class of its own. Peachleaf bellflowers are regal perennials that brighten up midsummer borders. There's nothing more stunning than a mix of blue and white bellflowers in the garden at sundown; they simply glow. While the plants may appear delicate, they do very well in prairie gardens and are easy to care for. Some staking is required to prevent flopping, however, and winter mulching is recommended. The long strap-like leaves of the plant are said to resemble those of peach trees (nothing we would know about here on the Prairies), hence its namesake. Peachleaf bellflowers adore rich organic soil, so compost should be regularly added throughout the growing season. While tolerant of full sun, these stately perennials perform best when shaded from the afternoon heat. Peachleaf bellflowers benefit from division every three to four years. Perfectly planted next to spring bulbs, they do a great job of covering up dead or dying foliage. One of the longest blooming of the summer perennials, the peachleaf bellflower is a definite must-have.

QUICK NOTES

Perennial Type: Herbaceous clumping border.

Top Choice Varieties: 'Alba' (white) and 'Chettle Charm' (white with blue edging).

Flower Colour and Type: Five-pointed bell-shaped blooms in pale blue or white.

Foliage Colour and Texture: Long, thin strap-like deep green leaves.

Size: Large—60-90 cm tall and 30-45 cm across.

Site Location: Peachleaf bellflowers like part sun and organic soil. Place these plants near the edge of borders where the blooms can be appreciated, or in mixed borders.

Perfect Partners: Beside yellow day lily, beebalm, or behind bigroot cranesbill.

Name/Origin/History: The word *campanula* in Latin means "bell-like" and *persicifolia* refers to the peach-like leaves of the perennial. Though not all bellflowers have a bell shape, many do. One idea about the origin of the Latin *campan* ("bell") is that the pronunciation "cam-pong" sounds much like "ding-dong" does in English. This may or may not be true. The plant's native range is Balkan Europe, extending as far east as Turkey.

Pros: This plant doesn't need much attention in order to thrive.

Cons: It may need staking to prevent it from flopping over.

Tips: Deadhead any fried flowers to ensure its continuous summer colour.

Bergenia
Bergenia cordifolia

Bergenia is one of the few plants that will happily exist in any condition from full sun to part shade, in dry or moist soil that is nutrient-rich or poor. This native of Siberia has been grown all over the world, in Mediterranean gardens as well as those of northern Saskatchewan. Now that's an adaptable perennial! Its shiny, rubber-like leaves make for a plant that can act alone as a feature plant or be grouped to create an effective ground cover. The plant's leaves are heart-shaped and evergreen, turning a bronze-red colour in the fall. The foliage becomes green soon after snows melt, producing stalks of small, bell-shaped blooms in early spring. Flowers come in red, magenta, pink, and white. Bergenia does well planted in groups under trees, as individual feature plants, or even planted in containers. The only caution about bergenia is because it's evergreen, cutting its leaves back in the fall will deter spring flowering. Avoid cutting back this plant if you can. If bergenia gets too big for its space, simply lift it up and divide it to create smaller plants. The more moisture this perennial receives, the larger it gets.

QUICK NOTES

Perennial Type: Evergreen clumping edger.

Top Choice Varieties: 'Bressingham Ruby' (reddish-pink).

Flower Colour and Type: Stalks of small, bell-like blooms in red, pink, magenta, and white.

Foliage Colour and Texture: Big, heart-shaped leathery leaves that are glossy green in spring, turning bronze-red in fall.

Size: Medium to large—30-45 cm tall and 60-90 cm across.

Site Location: Bergenia can be placed anywhere, but moist areas with part shade are best. It works great as an accent plant or at the front of a walkway where it gets noticed.

Perfect Partners: Near astilbes and fernleaf bleeding hearts.

Name/Origin/History: Bergenia is native to Siberia. Its genus is named after the eighteenth-century botanist Karl von Bergen, while *cordifolia* means "heart-shaped leaf."

Pros: Bergenia provides superior foliage for any garden condition.

Cons: Slugs can be a problem with this plant.

Tips: Divide plants every three to four years to rejuvenate it.

Bergenia is also known by the common name "pigsqueak" because of the high-pitched sound that occurs when thumb and forefinger are rubbed against the rubbery leaves of the plant.

PHOTO BY WINSTON GORETSKY

The name "blanket flower" comes from the bloom colours'
resemblance to the First Nations blankets of the American southwest.

Blanket Flower
Gaillardia x *grandiflora*

The blanket flower is another must have. Not only do these perennials offer vibrant two-toned colour in a daisy shape but they're also prairie natives. In fact, the wildflower species from which this hybrid comes can be found growing in highway ditches throughout Alberta, Saskatchewan, and Manitoba. Though late to emerge in the spring, blanket flowers offer a blast of colour to the late summer garden. The leaves are a mint-green colour and are the shape of a skateboard with jagged edges (similar to those produced by those funky-bladed scissors kids love). Blanket flowers will flop over when left to their own devices, so if an erect plant is your desire, staking is required. I, however, think the plants look equally good spilling into a lawn or path when placed near the front of a garden space. Though these plants have short garden lives, they can be easily divided in the spring, after which they will readily reseed. Since these are prairie plants, they don't need much attention and won't die if they're neglected when you leave on your summer vacation.

QUICK NOTES

Perennial Type: Herbaceous border.

Top Choice Varieties: 'Burgundy' (deep red), 'Fanfare' (yellow and red with fringed petals).

Flower Colour and Type: Often bicoloured daisy-like flowers in red, yellow, and orange.

Foliage Colour and Texture: Hairy oblong leaves with toothed edges in dull to medium green.

Size: Medium to large—20-60 cm tall and 20-60 cm across (check tags as sizes vary).

Site Location: Place blanket flowers in full sun. They will benefit from organic soil, but do fine in regular conditions where no additives are given. The plant performs decently in times of drought, though it readily drinks up water. However, it doesn't appreciate sitting in the wet stuff for too long.

Perfect Partners: Near 'Dragon's Blood' sedum and blazing star; in front of clematis.

Name/Origin/History: The blanket flower is native to the North American Prairies. Its botanical name pays honour to Gaillard de Marentonneau, an eighteenth-century French botanist and physician. *Grandiflora* simply means "big flowers."

Pros: The plant has a long bloom time.

Cons: It can suffer winterkill if its soil is too wet.

Tips: Deadheading will prolong the plant's blooming well into the fall.

Blazing star
Liatris spicata

Another prairie superstar, the blazing star should not go unnoticed. Structurally, this perennial has a lot of interest, with its feather-duster appearance, bright colour, and strap-like leaves. Unlike many other perennials, blazing stars bloom from the top down, giving the plants a mop-top look. Because of its overall unique look, it's best to use only one plant as a feature rather than planting en masse. Blooming begins in mid to late summer when tall spikes rise above the grassy leaves. Though they like the heat, blazing stars prefer rich organic soil that is well watered. Planting ground covers like moss phlox at the base of these plants will ensure that less water is lost to evaporation, and you won't have to water as often on hot days. Blazing star is also known by the common name "gay feather" and these blooms look great as cut flowers in arrangements. If more plants are desired, blazing star is easily divided in the spring. A magnet for both butterflies and bees, blazing star gives one the feeling of standing in a grassy meadow without having to leave home.

QUICK NOTES

Perennial Type: Herbaceous clumping perennial with tuberous roots.

Top Choice Varieties: 'Kobold' (purple), 'Alba' (white).

Flower Colour and Type: Purple or white fluffy spikes.

Foliage Colour and Texture: Spear-shaped leaves with a grass-like look in bright green.

Size: Large—50-90 cm tall and 30-45 cm across.

Site Location: Place blazing star in full to part sun in rich, moist soil. This plant generally doesn't suffer from hail damage as others might, and is a good choice for a more exposed area.

Perfect Partners: Beside coneflower, rudbeckia, and behind moss phlox.

Name/Origin/History: The blazing star is native to the eastern and central regions of North America. No one knows where the name *liatris* comes from, but *spicata* refers to the plant's spiky blooms. The common name "blazing star" refers to the comet-like appearance of the plant.

Pros: The blazing star needs little maintenance in order to look good.

Cons: It may occasionally contract powdery mildew and aphid infestations.

Tips: When blazing stars are finished blooming in the late summer/early fall, leave the expired blooms in place as they add winter interest to the garden.

Blazing stars are great as cut flowers and produce so many stalks that removing a few won't take away from the plant's impact.

*All bleeding hearts ('Luxuriant' pictured here) are
poisonous, making them unattractive to deer and rabbits.*

Bleeding Heart, Fernleaf
Dicentra formosa

This isn't your grandma's bleeding heart, it's better! The fernleaf bleeding heart is a superior plant for a number of reasons. First, unlike its bigger older cousin, the common bleeding heart (*D. spectabilis*), it doesn't turn yellow and go dormant in the summer. Second, this is a delicate tidy edger that doesn't grow to gigantic proportions and offers smaller fern-like foliage throughout the growing season. The fernleaf bleeding heart has a long flowering time, which extends from spring until late summer. These perennials perform best in moist organic soil in areas that receive full to part shade. The hotter and drier the area, the less flowering these plants do, so it's important to consider sheltered shaded sites. Fernleaf bleeding hearts don't like to be moved, so if you need to divide it, be careful when digging up the plant as the roots are very brittle. A closely related species, the fringed bleeding heart (*Dicentra exima*) is similar to the fernleaf but is native to Canada's east coast, making it less prairie-hardy. Looking fabulous in shaded areas, the fernleaf bleeding heart will surely make your garden visitors do a double take and say, "Is that what I think it is?"

QUICK NOTES

Perennial Type: Herbaceous edger.

Top Choice Varieties: 'Luxuriant' (red hybrid), 'Alba' (white).

Flower Colour and Type: Dangling heart-shaped flowers in red, pink, and white.

Foliage Colour and Texture: Fern-like leaves with a blue-green colour.

Size: Medium—30-40 cm tall and 40-60 cm across.

Site Location: Place fernleaf bleeding hearts in part to full shade.

Perfect Partners: Near coral bells and hosta.

Name/Origin/History: The fernleaf bleeding heart is native to wooded areas of the North American West Coast. The Latin word *dicentra* comes from the Greek *dis* ("twicc") and *kentron* ("spur"), which relates to the flower shape, while *formosa* translates to "beautiful." The common name for this plant makes sense when you look at its blooms.

Pros: This is a tough shade plant that is more drought-tolerant than the common bleeding heart.

Cons: The plant's brittle rhizomes snap easily, so handle its roots with care.

Tips: Plant these small bleeding hearts in groups of three for a lush effect.

Siberian bugloss ('Jack Frost' pictured here) should be planted in a shady, sheltered spot with lots of moisture, or it may develop scorched leaves.

Bugloss, Siberian
Brunnera macrophylla

While the word "Siberian" may evoke images of Stalinist-era gulags and misery to many, gardeners love perennials from this geographic region. Siberian plants thrive on the Prairies and bugloss is no exception. The year I fell in love with the 'Jack Frost' cultivar I knew I wasn't alone, after repeatedly spotting it during the Calgary Horticultural Society's annual garden competition tour. Much to my delight, it seemed to be everywhere! Few perennials combine elements of dark green and silver, but 'Jack Frost' does it beautifully. The leaves are hand-sized with a heart shape and only one is needed for your shade garden to sparkle. Though the foliage is the primary feature of this plant, the flowers are too cute for words. In late spring to early summer, tiny baby-blue flowers emerge on spikes just above the plant. These wee blooms resemble forget-me-nots, a common name regularly, yet incorrectly, given to bugloss. Not large in stature, Siberian bugloss is perfectly placed in rich organic soil at the edge of a border that is shaded for most of the day. While not readily available at smaller garden centres, if you see this plant, snatch it up quickly.

QUICK NOTES

Perennial Type: Herbaceous mounding edger that spreads by rhizomes.

Top Choice Varieties: 'Jack Frost' (variegated silver and green).

Flower Colour and Type: Tiny star-shaped bright blue blooms.

Foliage Colour and Texture: Variegated or green, big heart-shaped leaves with a felt-like texture.

Size: Medium—30-35 cm tall and 30-40 cm across.

Site Location: Plant bugloss in part to full shade in a moist, sheltered location.

Perfect Partners: Beside 'Othello' ligularia and 'Marmalade' coral bells.

Name/Origin/History: Bugloss is native to western Siberia and eastern Europe. Named after the eighteenth-century Swiss botanist Samuel Brunner, the word *macrophylla* is Greek for "big leaf." The word "bugloss" finds its roots in the Greek word for "ox-tongue," which the leaves were said to resemble.

Pros: This is a maintenance-free plant that looks great without effort.

Cons: It can be expensive to buy.

Tips: Deadhead bugloss regularly to prolong its blooming period.

Checker Mallow/Prairie Mallow
Sidalcea malviflora

If there's a perennial that deserves more attention than it gets, it's checker mallow. Resembling a miniature hollyhock, it's a great choice for those who love the look of the latter but have limited space. This perennial is completely hardy, and has an erect, tidy appearance and bright blooms in pink, red, purple, or white. Though some gardening books deem checker mallow to be finicky about soil and placement, I've found the plant to be one of the least demanding in my garden. Maybe it does so well on the Prairies because it is native to the mountains of western North America. Preferring hot days and cool nights, checker mallow is the perfect plant for gardeners in Alberta's foothills. While stunning as a single plant, if deadheading is halted throughout the summer, numerous babies will emerge the following spring, as it self-seeds like crazy. If the plant becomes shabby, cut it back and you'll be blessed with fresh growth and new blooms. Unlike its hollyhock cousin, checker mallow is longer lived but needs to be divided every three to four years to gain new vigour.

QUICK NOTES

Perennial Type: Herbaceous clumping border.

Top Choice Varieties: 'Brilliant' (bright red), 'Party Girl' (pink).

Flower Colour and Type: Small hollyhock-like blooms on upright spikes in pink, purple, white, and red.

Foliage Colour and Texture: Glossy green leaves with a deeply cut palmate shape.

Size: Large—50-120 cm tall and 40-60 cm across.

Site Location: Place checker mallow at the back of a mixed border in rich or average soil. This plant tolerates heat.

Perfect Partners: Beside rudbeckia, coneflower, globe thistle, and behind artemisia.

Name/Origin/History: The checker mallow is native to western North America. The Latin words *sidalcea* and *malviflora* give reference to the mallow family of plants, which includes hollyhocks and hibiscus or rose mallow. While I couldn't find source information for the word "checker," it probably refers to the circular shape of the flowers that resemble red checkers.

Pros: This plant produces bright blooms that like the heat.

Cons: It's prone to powdery mildew and aphid attacks.

Tips: Checker mallow is a major self-seeder. If you desire more plants, leave its flowers in place. Otherwise, deadhead, deadhead, deadhead.

*Checker mallow looks like a miniature hollyhock and
is a great addition to a low-maintenance garden.*

Clematis Vine

Clematis viticella (Italian or Hardy Type)
Clematis x *jackmanii* (Jackmanii Hybrid)

If you think that big flowering vines are a prairie pipe dream, think again. There are many types of clematis that do amazingly well in our climate. The trick is in knowing the difference between the clematises that thrive here and those that will die a slow (or sudden) and painful death. Keep in mind, if your clematis dies, it's not you, it's the plant (well, actually, it may be you, but I'm not going to say that because then you might toss this book). So how do you know which vines do well? The two types listed above are good choices to start with, the viticella being the thuggish parent of the hybrid jackmanii. The jackmanii has been listed along with the hardier Italian clematis because, depending upon where you live, this hybrid may be easier to find. The problem is that the jackmanii may not live as long as the Italian species and requires the application of mulch in the fall for winter protection. The plus side is that jackmanii vines grow like crazy and the blooms are spectacular. Jackmanii vines perform best when planted up against the house, while the Italian clematis can be planted anywhere in the garden that receives sun. The Italian vines don't need winter protection, either. Plant both clematis vines 10 cm deep to ensure they survive the winter, and you should be good to go. These vines are gorgeous, require little fuss, and will surely dazzle your garden visitors.

QUICK NOTES

Perennial Type: Herbaceous climbing vine.

Top Choice Varieties: Italian clematis— 'Etoile Violette' (bluish purple), 'Polish Spirit' (deep purple), Jackmanii hybrid—'Alba' (white), 'Superba' (deep purple).

Flower Colour and Type: Blue, purple, red, pink, and white in single or double varieties. Plant blooms are palm-sized and many jackmanii hybrids have shapes similar to five-petalled pinwheels.

Foliage Colour and Texture: Medium green, tear-drop-shaped leaves on twisting stalks.

Size: Extra-large—3 m tall and 1-2 m across.

Site Location: Plant clematises in sun or part sun in spots with moist, cool soil. These plants appreciate rich organic soil. Clematises need support in the form of a trellis, lattice, or fence. Velcro tape can be used to support tender vines.

Perfect Partners: Behind bigroot cranesbill and loosestrife.

Name/Origin/History: Italian clematis is native to southern Europe through to western Asia. The jackmanii hybrid was developed by British plant guy George Jackman (1801-1869) in the 1860s and is now one of the most popular clematis in North America. The word *clematis* is old Greek for "vine," while *viticella* means "small vine."

Pros: Clematis vines are easy to care for and grow quickly.

Cons: The plants can suffer from clematis wilt, which is a fungus that starts at the top of the plant and works its way down the vine, causing the stems to blacken. If you find your plant infected, remove any affected stalks quickly so it doesn't spread.

Tips: Cut the vines down in March or early April. This will ensure that the plant will grow with vigour in the spring. Leaving 6-10 cm of dead stalks on the plant will give new shoots a support to cling to before they reach your supporting latticework or trellis.

The adage that the clematis prefers "hot tops and cool feet" is only partially true. What these vines crave is the water that exists where the base is shaded. Clematis like the jack-manii (pictured here) flower in full sun whether or not they have their "feet" shaded.

Coneflower
Echinacea purpurea

These prairie natives are real performers. With coneflowers, the bloom show starts in late July and keeps on coming until the arrival of the first fall frost. Even when the blazing heat has passed and there's a slight chill in the air, these plants look great in the garden. The flower's cone-like centre is uniquely spiky and hard to the touch, which means it begs a finger-tapping, especially from children. A great alternative to the white shasta daisies that become limp in heat, the coneflower won't let you down. It's clump-forming, needs only to be divided every four years, and has few problems after it's established. Coneflowers like organic soil, and digging in compost around the plant's base during the spring and fall is a good idea. Butterflies love these plants, too, and if you plant this perennial, they will come. Occasionally, powdery mildew may be an annoyance, but proper site location and purchasing newer cultivars should reduce this risk. Even when soccer balls are kicked into them, these plants are resilient (I know from experience). The coneflower is a must-have for the prairie garden, and adds a splash of late-season colour to any sunny landscape.

QUICK NOTES

Perennial Type: Herbaceous clump-forming border.

Top Choice Varieties: 'Magnus' (magenta), 'White Swan' (white).

Flower Colour and Type: Daisy blooms in magenta-purple, deep pink, and white.

Foliage Colour and Texture: Hairy, spear-like leaves with grey-green colour. The plant has a bushy appearance.

Size: Large—45 cm-1 m tall and 40-60 cm across.

Site Location: Plant the coneflower in full sun with afternoon shade.

Perfect Partners: Beside blazing star, rudbeckia, and sage.

Name/Origin/History: The coneflower is native to the Prairies. Its botanical name is derived from the Greek *echinos* or "hedgehog" and refers to the spiky cone (coneflower) in the centre, while *purpurea* refers to its purple blooms.

Pros: Coneflowers produce big, beautiful blooms that tolerate summer heat.

Cons: It may contract powdery mildew, and the orange varieties aren't generally prairie-hardy.

Tips: Leave the plant's flower heads in place after they die to add winter interest.

Native to the Prairies, the coneflower was used by Aboriginal groups for its antibiotic properties. It's still commonly used (in pill form) to prevent colds and infections.

*Coral bells come in a variety of jazzy leaf
shapes and colours ('Cherries Jubilee' pictured here).*

Coral Bells
Heuchera sp.

Another perennial grown for its superior foliage, coral bells provide gardeners with bang for their buck. These plants form tidy mounds and offer ground cover without ever becoming invasive. As a feature plant, or in groups, coral bells offer shape, colour, and texture to the garden. Spikes of tiny bell-shaped flowers 30 cm tall emerge in late spring and last until midsummer. The leaves on coral bells are similar to annual geraniums (without the pungent smell), and are available in an array of colours in addition to green, including purple and amber. The darker green the leaves, however, the hardier the plant. This means that popular picks including 'Amber Waves,' 'Marmalade,' and 'Palace Purple' need protection and mulching in winter if they're going to survive. If you're willing to do it, these beauties are worth it. Tough thugs like 'Brandon Pink' and 'Northern Fire' need much less winter protection and aren't quite so picky. I once saw some 'Brandon Pink' coral bells looking healthy and flowering profusely while competing for space, sun, and water under a savin juniper in a totally exposed area. If they can do well in a situation like that, think of how well coral bells will do in your yard!

QUICK NOTES

Perennial Type: Evergreen clump-forming edger.

Top Choice Varieties: 'Amber Waves' (gold-green leaves with tiny light pink blooms), 'Obsidian' (purple-black leaves and tiny greenish-white blooms), 'Brandon Glow' (green leaves with tiny red blooms).

Flower Colour and Type: Small bell-shaped flowers appear on delicate-looking stalks in shades of red, pink, and white.

Foliage Colour and Texture: Leaves resemble annual geraniums in purple, bronze, amber, and green.

Size: Medium—45-60 cm tall and 30-45 cm across.

Site Location: Plant coral bells in part sun to part shade.

Perfect Partners: 'Northern Fire' and 'Palace Purple' look great together; in front of hosta or ligularia.

Name/Origin/History: Coral bells are native to western North America and are named after German physician Johann von Heucher (1677-1747). The term "alum root" comes from an alum-like astringent produced in the processing of coral bell roots, which were once used to treat small nicks and cuts.

Pros: Coral bells have great foliage that enhances the colour of other blooms.

Cons: Purple or amber varieties of the plant may not always be fully winter-hardy.

Tips: Plants shaded from the hot afternoon sun will have shinier leaves than those placed in full sun.

Cranesbill Geranium, Bigroot
Geranium macrorrhizum

If you only think of geraniums as odorous, scarlet-hued annuals in white plastic urns, think again. Geraniums, referred to as cranesbills because of the bird-like appearance of the flower's stamen, are also stunning prairie perennials. Cranesbill geraniums come in a variety of sizes and flower colours (all having the trademark geranium leaf shape), but in my opinion, the bigroot variety is the best. This perennial has a ton of appeal and looks great in any season. Plants form a neat mound and produce blooms in late spring to early summer. Bloom colours are available in pink, purple, and white and rise above the leaves on 6-cm stalks. In the late summer, the plants begin to change colour from a rich green to a bright orange-red. Bigroot cranesbills are fragrant, like their annual cousins, but tend not to be overpowering. A unique aspect of this plant is that big roots may appear above ground (the perennial spreads from rhizomes, though not invasively). Traditionally, cranesbills were gathered for their oils, which were used in medieval European medicine. Drought-tolerant once they're established, cranesbills are effective edgers that do a great job of suppressing weeds.

QUICK NOTES

Perennial Type: Semi-evergreen clumping ground cover with a mound shape.

Top Choice Varieties: 'Ingwerson's' (pale pink), 'Album' (white), 'Bevan's' (magenta).

Flower Colour and Type: Small five-petalled flowers in white, pink, and magenta.

Foliage Colour and Texture: Bright green leaves, turning to orange and red in the fall.

Size: Medium—25-60 cm tall and 45-60 cm across; stalks are 30-60 cm tall.

Site Location: Place bigroot cranesbills at the front of a border in sun to part sun; the soil should be organic and moist.

Perfect Partners: In front of rudbeckia, coneflower, and covering the base of clematis vine.

Name/Origin/History: This plant originates from southern France, Italy, Greece, and the Balkans. The Latin word *geranium* comes from the Greek *geranos* meaning "crane." The word *macrorrhizum* translates to "big root." The central parts of the plant's flower resemble the bill of a crane, hence its common name.

Pros: This is a neat, tidy perennial that needs little attention.

Cons: The aroma of the leaves can turn some people off this plant. Conduct a smell test before you buy them.

Tips: Don't panic if you see roots above the ground around this plant, as they spread from these rhizomes, which will eventually turn into new plants.

Bigroot cranesbill geraniums are an ideal choice because
they offer garden appeal in spring, summer, and fall.

Historically, creeping Jenny ('Aurea' pictured here) was used throughout Europe for its calming effect and as a hair dye.

Creeping Jenny, Golden/Moneywort

Lysimachia nummularia 'Aurea'

There's no other shade plant as versatile and tough as the golden creeping Jenny. This ground cover's leaves will brighten dark corners, and it also looks great as spilling filler in planters. The chartreuse leaves are great ground covers for shady areas and fill in quickly. Now, I know what you're thinking: If it's tough and spreads, it must be hard to control, right? Not really. The great thing about golden creeping Jenny is that it's easy to control if there's too much plant for your liking. Simply rip out the part of the plant you don't want and, voila. I often stick unwanted specimens into pots in the spring, and by late summer a waterfall of bright green is flowing over the container. Golden creeping Jenny is the preferred choice as compared to regular creeping Jenny, which is much more aggressive in prairie gardens. It's an economical choice, too, since only one small plant in the spring will turn into a decent-sized ground cover by late summer. Golden creeping Jenny is a perennial that will play a supporting-actor role to the larger main characters in your garden.

QUICK NOTES

Perennial Type: Semi-evergreen mat-forming ground cover.

Flower Colour and Type: Unimportant—small cup-shaped yellow flowers appear in late spring but are lost among the bright yellow-green leaves.

Foliage Colour and Texture: Chartreuse leaves that are soft to the touch and the size and shape of a penny.

Size: Small—5-10 cm tall and 30+ cm across.

Site Location: Plant golden creeping Jenny in part to full shade. It has no special soil requirements.

Perfect Partners: Looks great in containers with purple blooms, or planted under 'Obsidian' or 'Palace Purple' coral bells.

Name/Origin/History: Creeping Jenny is native to the wetlands of Europe and Russia. The Latin word *lysimachia* comes from the Greek for "ending of strife." The name honours King Lysimachos of Thrace (360-281 BCE), a Macedonian and contemporary of Alexander the Great (356-323 BCE). He is credited with calming down a bull with this plant. The word *nummularia* means "resembling coins," hence the plant's common name "moneywort."

Pros: This plant is easy to take care of and brightens up dark areas in the garden.

Cons: It's prone to slug attacks.

Tips: If these plants are used in containers, replant them in the garden in September to overwinter, so they may be used again in the spring without losing their size and shape. Creeping Jenny also spreads quickly by its rhizomes.

Day Lily
Hemerocallis spp.

Every Saturday gardener should own this plant. Few perennials exist that have tropical-like blossoms, glossy foliage, and the ability to be happy in almost every condition, but the day lily does just this. There are hundreds of cultivars in colours from black (really dark purple) to cream. While appearing delicate, these perennials are prairie-tough, and drought resistant to boot. Seldom, too, do pests or disease bother day lilies. As its common name implies, day lily blooms last for twenty-four hours, though a mature plant may have continuous flowering for a month during midsummer. Once a clump of day lilies is five years old and flowering fades, you'll need to divide it to rejuvenate it. This is best done in the early fall. Varieties come in all sizes, from the smallish 'Stella de Oro' (yellow), to the hedge-forming tawny day lily (orange), so be sure to check the plant tags carefully. It might be wise to warn new gardeners that most people don't stop at one day lily—they can quickly become an addiction.

QUICK NOTES

Perennial Type: Herbaceous clumping border.

Top Choice Varieties: 'Stella de Oro' (yellow), 'Bela Lugosi' (purple), 'Chicago Apache' (red).

Flower Colour and Type: Black (dark purple), purple, pink, red, mahogany, orange, yellow, and cream flowers that look like a cross between a lily and an orchid.

Foliage Colour and Texture: Shiny green strap-like leaves.

Size: Medium to extra-large—30-120 cm tall and 60-90 cm across.

Site Location: Plant day lilies anywhere, except in full shade. The more sun, the more blooms.

Perfect Partners: Near bellflower, coneflower, and globe thistle.

Name/Origin/History: Native to China, the day lily's name comes from the Greek *hemera* or "day" and *kallos* or "beauty." Though some sources claim that day lilies existed in Europe since the days of ancient Rome, others state the Chinese perennials entered the Mediterranean in the late sixteenth century. They became popular in North America in the 1890s.

Pros: The day lily is a beautiful flowering plant that isn't picky about placement.

Cons: Its blooms only last one day.

Tips: Deadhead the plant to ensure it doesn't waste energy on seed production.

In their native China, day lilies were regarded for their culinary uses, as well as their beauty. Eating the flowers was believed to strengthen a person's willpower ('Stella de oro' pictured here).

*The globe thistle offers bold and interesting structure to the garden
with both its spiny foliage and metallic-blue orb-like flowers.*

Globe Thistle
Echinops ritro

I developed an appreciation for thistles from my friend Frances "Xavier" Stewart, a native Nova Scotian. Being a prairie farm kid, I grew up detesting thistles and was puzzled when I learned Fran loved them. She had images of thistles everywhere and asked me once if I had any suggestions for garden-friendly varieties she could grow without the neighbours lynching her. Immediately, globe thistle came to mind. Though I normally wouldn't touch a thistle if my life depended on it, for Fran's sake, I decided to give it a try in my garden. I was pleasantly surprised. Globe thistle is an interesting plant that fills the back of a sunny border beautifully. Only one plant is needed for a small suburban garden, as these beauties can get big fast. The blooms are perfectly round and are bee magnets in the late summer when they emerge. Performing well in hot, dry locations where other perennials would fry, globe thistles are undemanding in terms of soil conditions and watering requirements once they're established. For uprooted Maritimers, and any prairie dweller crazy enough to like thistles, the globe variety is a must.

QUICK NOTES

Perennial Type: Herbaceous clumping border.

Top Choice Varieties: 'Veitch's blue' (steel blue).

Flower Colour and Type: Orb-like blooms in industrial blue and white.

Foliage Colour and Texture: Big grey-green thistle leaves.

Size: Large—60-90 cm tall and 60-90 cm across.

Site Location: Plant globe thistle in full sun in most soil conditions.

Perfect Partners: Close to 'Karl Foerster' reed grass and rudbeckia.

Name/Origin/History: Cultivated since the 1600s, globe thistle is native to central Europe through to central Asia. In its botanical name, *echinops* is Greek for "hedgehog" or "sea urchin," while *ritro* is probably an archaic term for "thorny plants." The term "globe thistle" is self-explanatory once you take a look at this perennial, though it's not actually a true thistle.

Pros: The globe thistle is very drought-resistant once established.

Cons: Aphids can be troublesome with this plant.

Tips: Make sure the globe thistle is given enough space, as it grows quickly. One plant is usually enough in an urban garden.

Grass, Blue Fescue
Festuca glauca

If there's one thing we can grow on the Prairies it's grass. This is probably why grasses are often overlooked as top choices for planting; they're just too common. Blue fescue shouldn't be ignored, however. It's an ornamental grass, forming near-bluish tufts that resemble the shape of Lisa Simpson's hair. It doesn't spread throughout the garden but stays nicely in place, showcasing the flowers of other plants or performing as an accent plant. In addition to its neat and tidy appearance, blue fescue is extremely drought-tolerant and needs very little care during heat waves. In June, this grass flowers, forming gold-coloured stalks that add more interest to garden beds. This perennial survives our winters well and little protection is required. Though some winter dieback may occur, in the spring, simply pull off the dead stuff and new growth will emerge. While fescues are often short-lived, they're easily divided for continued existence in your garden. Though not the best choice for planters, this grass looks great in the landscape near the front or edge of a sunny border.

QUICK NOTES

Perennial Type: Ornamental grass.

Top Choice Varieties: 'Elijah Blue' (silver-blue stalks), 'Skinner's Blue' (blue-green stalks).

Flower Colour and Type: Irrelevant, but golden grass plumes appear in midsummer.

Foliage Colour and Texture: Green-blue to steel-blue stalks.

Size: Medium—20 cm tall and 30 cm across.

Site Location: Plant blue fescue near the front or edge of a border in full to part sun in poor- to well-drained soil.

Perfect Partners: Beside 'Dragon's Blood' sedum, or planted en masse.

Name/Origin/History: Native to Eurasia, the word *festuca* is Latin for "grass stalk," while *glauca* refers to the silvery-whitish covering on the stems.

Pros: Blue fescue grass loves drought and heat.

Cons: It has a short lifespan, usually three to four years.

Tips: Cut off the plant's golden plumes if you wish to show off the blue of the grass more.

Many fescue grasses ('Elijah Blue' pictured here) are allelopathic, meaning that the roots prevent weed seeds from germinating. For the plant, this means fewer rivals; for gardeners, it means less work. Currently, it's still unclear whether or not blue fescue grasses possess allelopathic properties.

Karl Foerster, for whom this plant was named, was a German plant breeder with an interesting past. During World War II, he hired Jewish employees at his nursery and refused Nazi demands for creating and selling only "pure" German plants. He died in 1970 at the age of ninety-six.

Grass, 'Karl Foerster' Feather Reed
Calamagrostis x *acutiflora* 'Karl Foerster'

'Karl Foerster' feather reed ornamental grass is yet another perennial that shouldn't be overlooked. I know what you're thinking—"Who wants to grow boring old grass?"— but believe me, you'll love this plant. 'Karl Foerster' is tall, elegant, and minds its garden manners beautifully. One of the fears of growing any type of grass on the Prairies is what happens if it seeds all over the place and gets out of control? There's no need to worry about good ol' "Chucky F." spreading, as the seeds it produces are sterile. If you want more plants, simply lift and divide it in the spring. Karl looks great as an accent plant—a good thing, considering these plants can be pricey. The hardest thing to overcome when growing ornamental grasses is our prairie prejudice toward them. Farmers, especially, need to overcome their "grassism" and be reminded that it's okay to have some tall grasses like Karl in the flowerbeds. In other words, not all grass needs a shot of Roundup™! Remember: "Though quack is bad, Karl is rad." This grass looks great whether it's grown in small urban gardens, or found swaying freely out in a country setting. Lose your stereotypes and plant it!

QUICK NOTES

Perennial Type: Upright clumping ornamental grass.

Flower Colour and Type: Light pink plumes in spring that turn golden in the fall; blooms are feathery to the touch.

Foliage Colour and Texture: Grass-green leaves.

Size: Extra-large—40-45 cm across and 90-140 cm tall (Karl adds a lot of height without taking up much space).

Site Location: Plant Karl in full to part sun in average/organic soil. This plant likes compost.

Perfect Partners: Near coneflowers.

Name/Origin/History: 'Karl Foerster' is a hybrid developed by, you guessed it, German plant guy Karl Foerster (1874-1970). The Latin words *calamus* and *agrostis* translate to "reed grass," while *acutiflora* is Greek for "sharply pointed flower."

Pros: 'Karl Foerster' is an easy-growing grass that behaves itself and adds height.

Cons: The negative prairie stereotypes against ornamental grasses mean that this plant isn't as popular as it should be.

Tips: Karl is a perennial grass with four-season appeal. It looks great in the winter, so don't cut it down until spring.

Hens and Chicks
Sempervivum spp.

If an easy, interesting ground cover that minds its garden manners is what you're after, hens and chicks is your plant. This succulent is one of the most undemanding plants I've grown, and it also looks great in the landscape. Simply stick it in well-drained soil where it can be seen, give it a bit of water, and there's your perennial. Hens and chicks thrive in poor soils that drain easily; fertile heavy-clay soils are the only no-no for this plant. These perennials thrive in hot conditions and perform well in raised beds and containers. Hens and chicks typically come in shades of red and green, and are often two-toned. A "webbed" variety also exists, giving the illusion that spiders have made a home on your plant. Grown for its texture, when hens and chicks do bloom, you might think that an alien force has invaded your plant. A 30-cm stalk will shoot up from a single "hen" with star-like flower clusters, causing it to die. The "chicks," however, quickly take over, so the loss is minimal. Kids love this plant, so if it's accidentally pulled out by small hands, simply pop it into the ground and no damage is done.

QUICK NOTES

Perennial Type: Evergreen ground cover that forms tight clusters.

Flower Colour and Type: Not grown for flowers—individual plants die after flowering.

Foliage Colour and Texture: Fleshy leaves that are spiky to the touch. Webbed varieties are available and add interest. Available in shades of green and red.

Size: Small—10 cm tall and up to 30 cm across (per cluster).

Site Location: Plant hens and chicks in full sun at the front of a border, in containers, or in raised beds in poor, well-drained soil.

Perfect Partners: Near sedum and Whitley's Veronica/speedwell.

Name/Origin/History: Hens and chicks are native to the mountains of Europe. The word *sempervivum* means "to live forever." Hens and chicks are also known by the common name "houseleek," referring to its historical use on rooftops.

Pros: This is a very easy plant that needs little attention.

Cons: The plants die after blooming but are quickly replaced by their "young."

Tips: Plant hens and chicks where they won't be overpowered by the leaves of taller perennials.

Hens and chicks were used throughout medieval
Europe on cottage roofs to ward off lightning.

Hollyhocks (single-flowering 'Nigra' pictured here) were used in Europe to treat the swollen hocks of horses.

Hollyhock, Black
Alcea rosea 'Nigra'

If you think hollyhocks are mundane and worth only a yawn, think again. Over the past few years, gardeners have been anxious to add black (well, deep, dark purple, actually) to their landscapes. One perennial that offers this colouring is the hollyhock. 'Nigra' offers this uniqueness in a reliably hardy plant. Hollyhocks are commonly biennial, though perennial versions exist that are equally short-lived. The bonus is that these perennials seed like crazy, so new plants will emerge every year if allowed to do so. Both single and double types of flowers exist (blooming in July and August), though the doubles are generally less hardy. If you're lucky, mutant doubles may sometimes emerge from single-flowered seeds, offering some cool contrasts in the landscape. These plants are quite easy to care for, the only real concern being a susceptibility to rust, though this is less common with newer varieties like 'Nigra.' While impressive, these are big plants, and their size must be considered if space is a concern in your backyard. If you want dark colour in a tall plant, however, this is the one for you. Black hollyhocks are a great addition to a prairie garden and will make people visiting ask, "Is that flower really black?"

QUICK NOTES

Perennial Type: Herbaceous clumping border.

Top Choice Varieties: 'Nigra' (single), 'Negrita' (double).

Flower Colour and Type: Dark purple to near black; flowers come in single and double varieties.

Foliage Colour and Texture: Large deep green leaves with a felt-like feel.

Size: Large—1-2 m tall and 60-90 cm across.

Site Location: Plant hollyhocks in full to part sun in rich soil.

Perfect Partners: Beside day lilies.

Name/Origin/History: Originating from China, hollyhocks were introduced to Europe during the Crusades. Many believed the plant came from the Holy Land, hence the name "hollyhock." The word *alcea* is from the Greek word for "mallow" and *rosea* translates to "pink."

Pros: A stately addition to the back of a border, hollyhocks add "walls" to the garden.

Cons: The hollyhock needs staking, is short-lived, and is susceptible to slug damage and rust.

Tips: Allow some flowers to dry up and self-seed to ensure the plant continues in your garden every year.

Honeysuckle Vine, 'Dropmore Scarlet'

Lonicera x *brownii* 'Dropmore Scarlet'

If a tough flowering vine is what you're looking for, look no further than the 'Dropmore Scarlet.' Never needing much in terms of care, the Dropmore attracts a lot of attention when it starts to bloom in the summer around June. Its green leaves become heavily adorned with scarlet-hued trumpet-like flowers that continue well on into September. It makes a perfect screen to block out nosy neighbours and is great at adding height to the garden. Like many prairie thugs, the 'Dropmore Scarlet' honeysuckle was developed in Manitoba by the late great Canadian plantsman Frank L. Skinner (1882-1967). Dropmore vines grow quickly and will cover a trellis or an arch in a growing season. They cling to supports by means of twinning stems that twist together like the snakes on the Canadian Medical Association logo. The only pruning that's required is in removing dead or damaged foliage from the plant. The Dropmore is well-mannered, and it's easily contained if given enough support. Dropmore's flowers won't result in little climbers emerging all over the garden, either, as it's a hybrid. Frank Skinner certainly knew what he was doing in creating this gorgeous vine, and it continues to be one of the best prairie choices on the market.

QUICK NOTES

Perennial Type: Climbing vine.

Flower Colour and Type: Bugle-shaped reddish-orange flowers.

Foliage Colour and Texture: Oval deep green leaves.

Size: Extra-large—3-4 m tall and 1-2 m across.

Site Location: Plant 'Dropmore Scarlet' in full sun in a western or eastern exposure, surrounded by rich organic soil that is evenly moist. Make sure the vine is well supported by tying it to a trellis, lattice, or arbour. Velcro tape strips work well for securing it in place. Dropmore is a great accent plant, or it can provide a good backdrop for other perennials. Just give it enough room to spread.

Perfect Partners: Behind day lilies or coneflowers.

Name/Origin/History: 'Dropmore Scarlet' was developed in Manitoba. The Latin word *lonicera* in its botanical name is associated with sixteenth-century botanist Adam Lonitzer (1527-1586), while the word *brownii* honours the eighteenth-century Scottish plant explorer Robert Brown (1773-1858). The name "honeysuckle" refers to the sweet nectar deep within the flower.

Pros: Hummingbirds go crazy over this perennial and if you plant it they will come.

Cons: Don't even try dividing this one or you'll damage the root and wreck the plant.

Tips: This plant blooms on new growth. To encourage flowers in the spring, prune it close to the uppermost buds in the spring when new leaves are starting to uncurl.

The 'Dropmore Scarlet' honeysuckle is named after the village of Dropmore, Manitoba, close to Frank Skinner's farm. Skinner was one of Canada's best plant producers and developed over two hundred tough plant varieties for life on the Prairies.

*Vampires of the plant world, hostas ('Gold Standard' pictured here)
feel threatened by strong sunlight.*

Hosta
Hosta spp.

Looking for something to bring a touch of the tropics to your landscape? If so, hosta is your plant. Also known as plantain lily, this perennial not only tolerates shade, it loves it! Hundreds of hostas exist, and the leaf colour of the plant determines how many rays it will tolerate. The darker, or bluer, the leaf, the more shade the plant requires. Dark-leaved types like 'Big Daddy' and 'Sieboldiana Elegans' need shade, while light-coloured plants, including 'Sun Power' and 'August Moon,' will tolerate part sun. Hostas come in all shapes and sizes; their leaves may be narrow and spear-like, or huge and heart-shaped. All hostas love rich, organic, and moist soil. Make sure to dig in a generous amount of compost around the hosta each spring and late summer to keep it happy. If you're planting hostas in exposed sites, be careful; when hail hits (it will, unfortunately), your beautiful leaves will have an unsightly ripped appearance. While slugs are the hosta's biggest threat, they can be repelled using the copper wire method explained in Chapter 5. Though a tad finicky, many prairie gardeners adore hostas. At last count, I had twenty-one varieties in my yard.

QUICK NOTES

Perennial Type: Herbaceous clump-forming border.

Top Choice Varieties: 'Albo-marginata' (green with white edges), 'Frances Williams' (blue-green with golden edges), 'Gold Standard' (chartreuse with dark green edges).

Flower Colour and Type: Lavender or white tubular flowers that appear above the foliage.

Foliage Colour and Texture: Solid leaf colours range from gold to green, to blue-green, while variegated varieties may offer colour contrasts down the centre or around the edges of leaves.

Size: Medium to large—45-60 cm tall and 30-45 cm across.

Site Location: Darker-leaved hostas should be placed in the shade, while lighter-leaved varieties will tolerate part sun.

Perfect Partners: Beside astilbe and coral bells.

Name/Origin/History: Native to Korea, Japan, and China, the hosta was named after Dr. Nicholas Host (1761-1834), botanist and physician to Austrian Emperor Francis II.

Pros: The hosta thrives in the shade.

Cons: Slugs can be a problem, especially with young tender plants. Be ever vigilant!

Tips: If hail is on the way, protect your hostas with an umbrella placed lightly over individual plants.

Iris, Siberian
Iris sibirica

If there's a perennial that oozes elegance and images of Impressionist paintings, it's the Siberian iris. While many gardeners dislike the traditional beaded iris for its tendency to take up a lot of room and flop over, its Siberian cousin is different. This plant is tall and adds height to the garden without overtaking its neighbours. The foliage is strap-like, meaning that the plant still looks good after the flowers have faded, and the leaves are hail-resistant. While the plant's bloom period is short, three to four weeks in May and June, the colour of Siberian irises is stunning, and includes blue, indigo, and white varieties. Best placed in an area that gets full sun and lots of moisture, irises respond well to rich organic soil conditions, and look great around ponds and water features. While delicate in appearance, any plant with the name "Siberian" is going to be well adapted to life on the Prairies. The iris is also known as the fleur-de-lis, a symbol Canadians know intimately, due to its prominence on the Quebec flag and association with French history. Among the oldest of cultivated flowers (irises appear in Egyptian hieroglyphs), the Siberian version is a stunning addition to a moist, sunny border.

QUICK NOTES

Perennial Type: Tall clumping border.

Top Choice Varieties: 'Caesar's brother' (indigo blue), 'Butter and Sugar' (white/yellow).

Flower Colour and Type: Blue, purple, white, and yellow blooms are showy yet complex in form, consisting of both erect and falling petals.

Foliage Colour and Texture: Long bright green strap-like leaves.

Size: Large—60-90 cm tall and 35-45 cm across.

Site Location: Plant the Siberian iris in full to part sun in rich moist soil. It's well-suited for placement near ponds or water features.

Perfect Partners: Behind bigroot cranesbill geranium and coral bells.

Name/Origin/History: This iris is native to Siberia, Euope, and Asia. Iris was the Roman goddess of rainbows and Juno's messenger. It was said by the ancients that the colours of the sky were reflected in the iris's flower petals.

Pros: This is a long-lived perennial.

Cons: This plant has a short bloom time that often occurs when people are on vacation and away from home (two weeks in midsummer).

Tips: Shear back dead foliage in the fall to encourage early spring growth.

The rhizomes of irises ('Silver Edge' pictured here) were used by the ancient Greeks and Romans to make perfume.

A common name attributed to lamb's ear is "woundwort," as the leaves of the plant were once used as bandages. The leaves are also said to relieve the pain of bee stings.

Lamb's Ear

Stachys byzantina

Fans of silver foliage will love this plant, as will people who frequently forget to water. Lamb's ear is an interesting perennial, to say the least. The leaves have the feel of, well, the ear of a young sheep, making this plant a magnet for kids who want to touch it. The plant has great foliage that superbly shows off the flowers of other perennials, and interesting spikes that bloom pink or purple in August. Its blooms, however, aren't what make this perennial attractive to many growers. Some types like 'Silver Carpet' seldom flower at all, and are purely grown for their foliar look and fuzzy feel. Lamb's ear performs well in drought conditions, in poor sandy soil that drains quickly. The only bane of lamb's ear is rich moist soil; the plant will die if exposed to winter wetness or if watered too much. It needs to be divided every three to four years, or when the middle of the plant looks dead. If you're looking for a plant that thrives in the heat and doesn't mind being missed by the watering wand, lamb's ear is a great choice.

QUICK NOTES

Perennial Type: Semi-evergreen ground cover that spreads from rhizomes.

Top Choice Varieties: 'Silver Carpet' (doesn't produce flowers—used for foliage only).

Flower Colour and Type: Insignificant; spikes of pink or purple.

Foliage Colour and Texture: Silver leaves with a spoon-like shape and fuzzy, papery texture.

Size: Medium—45-60 cm tall and 40-60 cm across.

Site Location: Plant lamb's ear in hot, dry locations in poor, well-drained soil; it's good for exposed raised beds.

Perfect Partners: Beside stonecrop and thrift.

Name/Origin/History: Lamb's ear is native to Turkey. In its botanical name, *stachys* translates to "flower spikes," while *byzantina* refers to Byzantium, an ancient Greek town that later became Constantinople, and is now Istanbul.

Pros: Lamb's ear is very drought-tolerant once it's established.

Cons: It may experience winter dieback if it becomes waterlogged.

Tips: Uncovering mulch from around the base too early in the spring may actually set back lamb's ear by exposing it to cold temperatures prematurely. Ensure that it's adequately protected for winter.

Lamium/Deadnettle
Lamium maculatum

If you're looking for a no-maintenance ground cover/edger for a shaded area, lamium is your plant. Lamium is a great filler plant if you want to conceal a bare space quickly. If you end up getting more plant than you like, simply rip out what you don't need. The foliage is gorgeous, and will surely lighten up dull spots in the shade. The flowers are similar to snapdragons and come in purple, magenta, and white. The common name "deadnettle" is attributed to lamium because it's said to resemble the stinging nettle plant in form, but without the itchiness. Lamium flowers bloom in late spring to summer. To give it a neater appearance, lamium should be given a good buzz once its petals fall. Another bonus of lamium is that it's a good choice for growing under trees, as it's highly adaptable and doesn't need much fuss. Its only requirement is that it has moist soil and at least some degree of shade throughout the day. Lamium is a no-worry plant that looks great all on its own or with other shade-lovers.

QUICK NOTES

Perennial Type: Herbaceous edger or ground cover.

Top Choice Varieties: 'Aureum' (yellow leaves with purple flowers), 'Beacon Silver' (silver leaves with green edges and magenta flowers), 'White Nancy' (silver leaves with green edges and pure white flowers).

Flower Colour and Type: Similar to snapdragon blooms in pink, purple, magenta, and white.

Foliage Colour and Texture: Mint-shaped leaves are the size of a loonie, with a slightly rough feel.

Size: Small to medium—15-20 cm tall and 60+ cm across.

Site Location: Plant lamium in part to full shade in an evenly moist location.

Perfect Partners: In front of hosta, astilbe, or fernleaf bleeding heart.

Name/Origin/History: This plant is native throughout Europe. *Lamium* in Latin means "dead nettle," while *maculatum* translates to "spotted."

Pros: Lamium is an easy shade plant that slugs, deer, and rabbits tend to hate.

Cons: It may grow too quickly under ideal conditions.

Tips: Cut back lamium hard after it's done blooming to keep it tidy.

*Lamium ('Aureum' pictured here) has been cultivated in Europe
for centuries, and was painted in the eighteenth century by the
father of botanical names, Carolus Linnaeus (1708-1778).*

Ligularia ('Othello' pictured here) has more common names than most perennials, including rayflower, elephant ears, golden ray, and golden groundsel. When in doubt, just say "ligularia."

Ligularia, Bigleaf
Ligularia dentata

For anyone wishing to add big bold leaves to their landscape, ligularia is a good choice. These plants are sure to add punch to a shaded landscape where hostas and bugloss also reside. Ligularia offers daisy-like flower clusters in dark yellow or orange during the peak of summer that form on tall stalks above its foliage. The leaves of this plant are kidney-shaped in appearance and absolutely huge compared to other prairie perennials. They prefer rich organic soil that stays evenly moist and is shaded for most of the day. If you choose to include ligularia in your garden, make sure hot, sunny spots are avoided. The leaves will wilt in direct sunlight, but once shade or evening hits, they rebound quickly to their original form. It's important to place these perennials in deep soil, as they don't perform well in shallow raised beds. An alternative to the bigleaf species, 'The Rocket' (*L. stenocephala*), has yellow spiky blooms and triangular jagged-edged leaves. Bigleaf ligularia is a plant with a lot of drama, which is probably why the names 'Othello' and 'Desdemona' (Shakespearean characters) are given to two popular varieties.

QUICK NOTES

Perennial Type: Herbaceous clumping border.

Top Choice Varieties: 'Othello' (purple-green leaves), 'Britt-Marie Crawford' (dark purple leaves).

Flower Colour and Type: Clusters of daisy-like blooms with fuzzy centres in yellow and orange.

Foliage Colour and Texture: Big kidney-shaped leaves with jagged edges.

Size: Large to extra-large—90-120 cm tall and 60-90 cm across.

Site Location: Plant ligularia in a moist border; it's a good choice near ponds. Avoid planting it in hot, sunny areas.

Perfect Partners: Near hosta, and behind coral bells.

Name/Origin/History: Native to China, *ligularia* means "like a small strap" in Latin, referring to the flower's petals, while *dentata* means "tooth-like," in reference to its leaf shape.

Pros: Ligularia provides dramatic foliage that adds height and interest to the garden.

Cons: Slugs love this plant and can quickly defoliate it.

Tips: Planting shade-loving ground covers like lamium and golden creeping Jenny at the plant's base will help prevent against midday moisture loss.

Lily, Asiatic
Lilium hybrids

Loving lilies as I do, I was overjoyed when I found out in 2006 that a University of Saskatchewan (my alma mater) lily had been developed. Now, when I view my U. of S. lily, I'm reminded of spring lunches in the Bowl and coffee breaks in Place Riel. There's nothing more pleasing than a newly blooming lily. Several species of lily perform well on the Prairies, but none can really compare to the Asiatic types, of which the U. of S. lily is a fine example. These perennials simply adore our prairie climate, and the blooms are the proof. Available in every colour but blue, and an astonishing assortment of pattern combinations, it's little wonder that lilies are globally so popular. Flower shapes come in diverse sizes, too, and may be upward, downward, or sideways facing. The leaves also add to the perennial's interest, as they're sword-like and jut out from the sides of the stems. Lilies emerge in the spring from bulbs, although an easy, inexpensive way of getting summer lilies is to plant the bulbs nose-down in a desired garden spot in mid- to late-September. Unlike other perennials, lilies actually prefer our cold winters, so the fall-planted bulbs won't mind the chill.

QUICK NOTES

Perennial Type: Bulb-forming clumping border.

Flower Colour and Type: All colours except blue, some with fragrance, with upward, downward, or sideways blooms (check plant tags for specifics).

Foliage Colour and Texture: Glossy green leaves that are narrow and jut out from the sides of the stem.

Size: Medium to large—30-120 cm tall and 30-45 cm across (check tags as sizes vary).

Site Location: Plant the lily in organic, well-drained soil in a site that gets full to part sun during the day. Lilies like to have cool roots, so planting ground covers near their base is a good idea.

Perfect Partners: Plant behind bigroot cranesbill and near peachleaf bellflower.

Name/Origin/History: While the species is native to China, lily hybridizers have dramatically changed the appearance of these lilies, and almost every Asiatic lily sold is a hybrid. Prairie lily hybridizers who were instrumental in the development of tough lilies include Frank Skinner (1882-1967), C. F. Patterson (1892-1961), and Bert Porter (1901-2000). These plant pioneers worked hard at developing the beautiful yet hardy lilies we grow today.

Pros: The Asiatic lily is a true pairie toughie.

Cons: This plant can suffer from botrytis.

Tips: Lilies are said to be toxic to cats, so beware if you have felines that stroll in the garden.

Lilies ('University of Saskatchewan' variety pictured here) have been cultivated for over three thousand years and are symbolic in Christianity, often relating to purity and the Virgin Mary.

Yellow loosestrife ('Alexander' pictured here) is closely related to golden creeping Jenny, though the two plants look nothing alike.

Loosestrife, Yellow
Lysimachia punctata

While I tend to avoid yellow flowers (probably because of something hidden deep in my subconscious), I fell in love with this perennial when I first spotted it during a trip to the Calgary Zoo. The yellow star-shaped blooms compare to the colour found only in a box of crayons; they are that rich in appearance. The foliage, too, offers super appeal, especially the variegated variety known as 'Alexander.' The plant is so strikingly unique that one of my garden visitors once asked, "Dawn, if you're a gardener, why do you have fake plants in your yard?" I had to convince this person that indeed the plant was real by breaking off a leaf. Yellow loosestrife comes in green and purple-leaved varieties as well, and all have the same flowers. It must be noted that yellow loosestrife shouldn't be confused with the dreaded invasive purple loosestrife, a noxious weed in Alberta that invades wetlands and chokes out native prairie slough plants. The two plants aren't related, so don't worry if you want to grow yellow loosestrife in your yard. Though this perennial can be vigorous in warmer areas of Canada, on the Prairies it is much less so because of our cold winters. A great feature plant sure to be a conversation piece in your yard, yellow loosestrife is a worthy choice.

QUICK NOTES

Perennial Type: Herbaceous clumping border.

Top Choice Varieties: 'Alexander' (variegated white and green leaves).

Flower Colour and Type: Yellow star-shaped blooms the size of a quarter.

Foliage Colour and Texture: Oval-shaped variegated green or purple leaves.

Size: Medium to large—40-75 cm tall and 40-60+ cm across.

Site Location: Plant yellow loosestrife in part sun in moist organic soil. Don't let this one dry out. It looks great as a feature plant or grouped with others.

Perfect Partners: Near peachleaf bellflower, or in front of bigroot geraniums.

Name/Origin/History: Yellow loosestrife is native to central Europe and east to Turkey. The Latin *lysimachia* means "to release or lose strife" (see previous creeping Jenny entry for full description), while *punctata* means "spotted."

Pros: This plant, especially 'Alexander,' is an interesting feature plant.

Cons: Nonvariegated varieties of loosestrife may be overly vigorous if conditions are ideal.

Tips: Make sure variegated varieties are fully mulched over the winter, as they aren't as tough as the green-leaved varieties.

Maltese Cross
Lychnis chalcedonica

While often labelled "too ordinary" by many experienced gardeners (my mother, for example), those new to the hobby often marvel at the interest this perennial offers. Maltese cross has become a staple in prairie gardens for good reason: it likes it here. In July, the blooms begin and last until August. Unlike its close relative, rose campion, Maltese cross benefits from deadheading, and has a longer garden lifespan than its cousin. The plant produces a flat dome of many tiny orange-red cross-shaped flowers that rise up on tall stalks. It's best placed near the back of a border because of its size and because it may need staking early on in the season. While not overly picky about soil, Maltese cross likes evenly moist conditions in full or part sun. Though white and pink varieties are available, in my opinion, red is the preferred colour as the others are much less showy. This is not a perennial that benefits from mass planting in small areas, as its colour can become overpowering. Maltese cross is easy to care for, not prone to diseases, and thrives in our region; what more could you ask for?

QUICK NOTES

Perennial Type: Herbaceous clumping border.

Flower Colour and Type: Tiny red and orange-red cross-shaped blooms in a domed cluster.

Foliage Colour and Texture: Bright green narrow leaves with a slightly hairy feel.

Size: Large—90-120 cm tall and 25-30 cm across.

Site Location: Plant Maltese cross near the back of a mixed border in average soil in full to part sun.

Perfect Partners: Near 'May Night' sage.

Name/Origin/History: Native to Russia, it was believed Maltese cross was brought to Europe during the Crusades by the Knights of Malva.

The word *lychnis* in its botanical name means "lamp" (see rose campion, p. 136), while *chalcedonica* refers to the ancient port town of Chalcedon, Turkey, now part of Istanbul.

Pros: Maltese cross is a tall, stately plant that has few enemies.

Cons: It may be prone to wind damage if it's improperly staked. Leafcutter bees cutting out half circles in the leaves can quickly wreck the appearance of the plant's foliage.

Tips: Make sure Maltese cross isn't planted next to other bright red or pink blooms, as its impact may be lost in a sea of colour.

*Lychnis plants, like Maltese cross (pictured here) were mentioned
in the writing of Theophrastus (c. 372-287 BCE), an ancient Greek
botanist and contemporary of Aristotle (384-322 BCE).*

The petals of the pasque flower were once used in
its native Europe to make green Easter egg dye.

Pasque Flower
Pulsatilla vulgaris

There's nothing that says spring like the blooms of the pasque flower. Often emerging through the last bit of snow on the ground, this plant is among the first to bloom in prairie gardens, often in late April. The pasque flower is extremely hardy and loves our climate. Its ferny foliage is quite attractive when it pops out of the ground, followed by its bright-coloured flowers. After the blooms have faded, the plant produces interesting seed heads that resemble images from a Dr. Seuss book. While not hugely particular about where it's placed (though it likes full sun and dislikes standing in water), these perennials detest being moved around. Take some time to think about where you want it before you stick it any old place. Often reblooming in the fall, this perennial has lots of appeal, which is probably why the red cultivar 'Rubra' is the official flower of Calgary. These plants tend to last a long time in the garden—a bonus, since division is difficult. A staple of rock gardens, the pasque flower looks great at the edge of borders where their bright colour and foliage can be enjoyed. A cousin to our native prairie crocuses that adorn pasture land, the pasque flower is a definite must-have.

QUICK NOTES

Perennial Type: Clumping herbaceous edger.

Top Choice Varieties: 'Alba' (white), 'Red Clock' (bright red).

Flower Colour and Type: Purple, white, and red palm-sized blooms.

Foliage Colour and Texture: Light green fern-like leaves.

Size: Medium—15-40 cm tall and 15-30 cm across.

Site Location: Plant the pasque flower in full to part sun, near the front of a border in fertile soil that drains easily.

Perfect Partners: Beside cushion spurge and 'Autumn Joy' sedum.

Name/Origin/History: The pasque flower is native to central Europe. In its botanical name, *Pulsatilla* refers to the plant's habit of pulsating in the wind, while *vulgaris* means "common" in Latin. The name "pasque flower" refers to the fact that it blooms around Easter (of course, it blooms later on the Prairies).

Pros: The pasque flower is among the first flowers to emerge in the spring, and they also have four-season interest.

Cons: This plant may be prone to aphid attacks.

Tips: Leave some dead flowers in place on the plant for the desired Dr. Seuss effect.

Peony, Garden
Paeonia lactiflora

For those who think it impossible to grow big blossoms on the Prairies, I have one word: peonies. While the blooms appear for only a few weeks in June or July, they're well worth it. Needless to say, peonies are very long-lived, often continuing to thrive undisturbed for eighty or more years. Even when disturbed, they'll often thrive. My mom tells a story about my dad rototilling the garden and taking some peonies out in the process, only to have them emerge again the following spring. Now that's a tough plant! The blooms of these plants are big and bold and come in single and double varieties. Many peonies also offer passersby a pretty perfume scent. Checking the plant tags will tell you whether or not your plant will offer more or less aroma. Another bonus is the foliage. After the blooms on a peony fade, a neat, tidy shrub-like plant is left, with leaves that often turn red in the fall. All of this, combined with the fact that it likes clay soil, makes the garden peony the perfect prairie plant.

QUICK NOTES

Perennial Type: Herbaceous shrub-like clumping border perennial.

Top Choice Varieties: 'Karl Rosenfield' (double red), 'Sarah Bernhardt' (double pink).

Flower Colour and Type: Massive single or double fragrant rose-like blooms in white, pink, red, and yellow.

Foliage Colour and Texture: Glossy green narrow leaves that turn red in the fall.

Size: Large—60-120 cm tall and 60-100 cm across.

Site Location: Plant peonies in full sun in fertile soil. They look great as a hedge or as accent plants.

Perfect Partners: Beside other peonies!

Name/Origin/History: The peony is native to China, Tibet, Siberia, and Mongolia. The Latin word *paeonia* comes from the Greek word *pai nia*, referring to Paion, who was Zeus's doctor. The word *lactiflora* means "with milk-coloured flowers."

Pros: Peonies are all about the blooms!

Cons: Peonies may be prone to botrytis.

Tips: When planting peonies, make sure their roots aren't planted too deep or the plants may not bloom. Staking peonies with a hoop-type support is needed because the flowers are heavy.

Peonies ('Kansas' pictured here) have been constants in prairie gardens since homesteading days. It's not uncommon to find them flowering in farmyards abandoned since the Depression.

Periwinkle vine ('Variegata' pictured here) has been used in European medicine for centuries and contains up to seventy different types of alkaloids.

Periwinkle Vine
Vinca minor

I fell in love with this plant the first time I saw it bloom in the garden. Periwinkle vine is a great ground cover for partly shaded areas that are close to the house or other heated structures that offer these plants a bit of protection during the winter. While periwinkle can become an invasive pest in warmer areas of North America, on the Prairies, it minds its manners well. This isn't a plant you want to leave exposed to the elements, however, when placed in the right area, it doesn't need much in terms of extra care. The variegated varieties are generally less vigorous than the green-leaved varieties. Pinwheel-shaped blooms appear in early spring in a flush of blue, and then sporadically throughout the growing season. One of the great things about this ground cover is that it doesn't appear to be bothered by slugs. It's one of the few shade-liking perennials I have that isn't covered with slime during the late summer nights. Another bonus of periwinkle is that it looks great trailing over the edge of pots. Then, in the late summer, these ground vines can be replanted in the garden.

QUICK NOTES

Perennial Type: Creeping ground cover.

Top Choice Varieties: 'Illumination' (yellow leaves with green edges and blue flowers), 'Alba' (white flowers).

Flower Colour and Type: Small pinwheel-shaped blooms in blue and white.

Foliage Colour and Texture: Oval-shaped quarter-sized leaves that are solid green or variegated.

Size: Small to medium—5-15 cm tall and 45-60 cm across.

Site Location: Plant periwinkle in spots that are shaded from the afternoon sun (in sheltered locations like near the house) in evenly moist organic soil.

Perfect Partners: In front of coral bells or fernleaf bleeding heart.

Name/Origin/History: Periwinkle vine is native throughout southern Europe. The word *vinca* in its botanical name means "to bind," while *minor* means "lesser." The name "periwinkle" is of unknown origin.

Pros: Periwinkle isn't bothered by pests or diseases.

Cons: If this plant is exposed to the elements, its leaves and stems will turn brown and dry out.

Tips: These plants are easily pulled apart and replanted if more are required.

Phlox, Moss
Phlox subulata

Before I started gardening, I had a mental image that small plants were weak and delicate. Moss phlox made me change my opinion. This is one of the toughest little plants out there. My brightly coloured moss phlox was the first perennial I ever bought (before I even knew what a perennial was), and it has been a constant in my yard ever since. The vibrant blooms appear in the spring over a mound of needle-like leaves. You can gently cut back the spent blooms after its spring flowering for a tidier look. You'll need to divide it every four years, which is best done in the fall when the leaves turn a bronze colour. Another top phlox, if you can get your hands on it, is 'Douglas phlox' (*Phlox douglasii*), which forms a small dome and explodes with blooms in the summer. Neither phlox needs much mulching or attention to prepare it for harsh prairie winters. That said, phlox detests wet soil, which causes its roots to rot. Buy phlox plants early in the spring, place them in a sunny spot that isn't wet, and wait for the blooming bonanza to begin. If you like what you see, next year will be even better!

QUICK NOTES

Perennial Type: Evergreen mat-forming ground cover.

Top Choice Varieties: 'Candy Stripe' (white with pink striping).

Flower Colour and Type: Small star-shaped blooms in white, pink, red, and lilac; blooms are sometimes bicoloured.

Foliage Colour and Texture: Needle-like medium green leaves.

Size: Small—5-15 cm tall and 30-50 cm across.

Site Location: Plant moss phlox in part to full sun in a location that drains well—avoid planting it in wet areas.

Perfect Partners: Near sedum and pussytoes.

Name/Origin/History: Native throughout North America, the word *phlox* means "flame," while *subulata* translates to "awl-shaped," referring to the plant's sharp, pointy leaves.

Pros: Unlike the taller garden phlox, diseases or pests seldom bother this species.

Cons: Moss phlox can experience winter dieback when exposed to wet conditions.

Tips: Cut moss phlox back a lot after it flowers in the spring to tidy it up. By doing so, you may also get a fall flush of flowers

Moss phlox ('Scarlet Flame' pictured here) is native to Canada, and became highly prized by early explorers and botanists, eager to grow the colourful New World plant in European gardens.

Cheddar pinks ('Firewitch' pictured here) are named in honour of Cheddar Gorge in the United Kingdom, a place also known for its good cheese.

Pinks, Cheddar, Maiden

Dianthus gratianopolitanus, D. deltoides

I remember going to a friend's house once and commenting on the gorgeous pinks in her garden. Eagerly, my girlfriend grabbed me and whispered out of earshot of the others, "You know what Dawn, I didn't do anything to them, and they look this good; I don't even water them!" That's pinks for you. These perennials are among my favourites. They have vibrant carnation-like blooms, with a baking-spice scent. The larger of the two, Cheddar pinks, form a small mound, while the petite maidens create a grassy mat with tiny thumbnail-sized flowers. Though quite short-lived (three to four years), pinks easily self-seed, so don't get rid of all the dead flowers. Pinks do well in full sun, shine in the heat, and perform well with limited watering. Mulching is not required, as these perennials detest rich, moist spots. All of these factors, combined with the fact that pinks tolerate alkaline soil quite well, make for a superbly prairie-adapted perennial.

QUICK NOTES

Perennial Type: Evergreen mat- and mound-forming ground cover.

Top Choice Varieties: Cheddar pinks— 'Firewitch' (hot pink) and 'Tiny Rubies' (double pink); Maiden pinks— 'Flashing Light' (magenta) and 'Arctic Fire' (white with red eye).

Flower Colour and Type: Fragrant blooms in many shades of pink, red, and white, including bicolours with a five-petalled carnation-like look.

Foliage Colour and Texture: Cheddar pinks—grassy look in a mound form with a steel-blue colour; Maiden pinks—grassy look in a mat form with a green colour.

Size: Small—10-30 cm tall and 20-40 cm across (check tags as sizes vary).

Site Location: Plant pinks in full to part sun in well-drained soil. While they don't require rich soil, they benefit from rock mulch or coverage. Avoid planting sites that get overly wet in the winter.

Perfect Partners: Near lamb's ear, artemisia, and other pinks.

Name/Origin/History: Both species of pinks are native to Europe. Their botanical name *dianthus* in Greek means "flower of the gods" and was used by the ancient philosopher Theophrastus. The Latin word *deltoides* means "triangle-shaped," while the exact origin of the name "maiden" couldn't be found. The Latin word *gratianopolitanus* refers to the region of Grenoble, France, part of the plant's home range.

Pros: Pinks are easy perennials that aren't bothered by pests or disease.

Cons: Pinks may experience winter dieback if their soil is moist in the winter. They also have a short lifespan (three to four years).

Tips: Nonhybrid pinks tend to self-seed like crazy, and considering their short lifespan, it's a good idea to keep some flower heads in place during the summer.

Poppy, Iceland
Papaver nudicaule

Before becoming a serious gardener, I assumed all poppies were tall and overpowering, so I avoided planting them. How wrong I was. Iceland poppies are the ideal choice for people who like poppies but are turned off by the idea of them taking up a lot of garden space. These poppies are diminutive, yet they add a punch of spectacular colour. While traditional oriental types (the larger vibrant poppies many Saturday gardeners may be familiar with) can be overpowering in a postage-stamp-sized suburban garden, the Icelandic variety offers a great alternative. It may be correctly assumed, from its geographic labelling, that the perennial will adapt well to prairie gardens. While these small poppies are tolerant of the cold, they don't have long garden lives (two to three years). That said, these brilliant bloomers seed like crazy, so if you leave them alone, more new poppies are almost guaranteed to emerge the following spring. Iceland poppies work well to fill in garden gaps as accent plants or in a group of three near the front of a sunny border. Wherever placed, they will certainly add spark with their bold colour and paper-like blooms.

QUICK NOTES

Perennial Type: Herbaceous clumping edger that should be treated as a biennial.

Top Choice Varieties: 'Champagne Bubbles' (vibrant array of colours on short, stocky plants).

Flower Colour and Type: Bright cup-shaped palm-sized blooms in red, salmon, pink, orange, yellow, and white.

Foliage Colour and Texture: Grey-green foliage with jagged leaves with a coarse hairy feel.

Size: Medium—30-40 cm tall and 15-30 cm across.

Site Location: The Iceland poppy tolerates average to poor soils and is drought-tolerant. Plant it in full to part sun, near the front of the garden.

Perfect Partners: Beside bigroot cranesbill, or in front of peachleaf bellflower.

Name/Origin/History: The Iceland poppy is native to the subpolar regions of Europe. The botanical name *papaver* is from the Latin word "pap," meaning "milky juice," referring to the plant's white sap. The word *nudicaule* means "with leafless stems." The name "poppy" comes from the Anglo-Saxon word "popig," or "to sleep," referring to the morphine-like effect the extracts of many poppy plants can produce.

Pros: This plant makes you look like a great gardener without even trying.

Cons: The Iceland poppy has a short lifespan (two to three years). Since these plants are sold as mixtures, you may not know what colour you're getting until blooming begins.

Tips: Iceland poppies don't like having their roots upset, so this isn't a plant that should be moved around.

Poppies have been cultivated for over five thousand years,
their images appearing in ancient Egyptian tombs.

Pussytoes ('Rosea' pictured here) originate from native prairie
plants commonly seen growing in pastures and having white flowers.

Pussytoes

Antennaria rosea

I had déjà vu the first time I saw pussytoes in a garden centre. The next time I visited my brother's farm I learned why; the native versions of this plant were growing in his yard. Like coneflowers, pussytoes are a tamed version of a highly adaptable native prairie plant that offers reliability without military-like garden aggression. These low-growers form clumps of silvery green woolly foliage that show off the globe-shaped clustered blooms that resemble the pads of a cat's foot, hence the common name. Pussytoes start blooming in June, after which, blooming lasts for several weeks. Once done flowering, pussytoes should be cut back hard; this perennial actually tolerates being mown. The only problem I've ever experienced with this plant was an ant invasion one year that turned out to be more of a nuisance than anything else. Pussytoes look impressive planted along paving stones, or in a small clump near the front of a garden border. Extremely tough with respectable garden manners, pussytoes are a welcome addition to any prairie garden.

QUICK NOTES

Perennial Type: Evergreen mat-forming ground cover.

Top Choice Varieties: 'Rosea' (dark pink).

Flower Colour and Type: Small round blooms appear in clusters on stems that rise 10-15 cm above the leaves.

Foliage Colour and Texture: Small grey-green spoon-shaped leaves with a woolly texture.

Size: Small—5-10 cm tall and 30+ cm across.

Site Location: Plant pussytoes in full sun in average to poor soil at the front edge of the garden or near paving stones.

Perfect Partners: Near stonecrop, hens and chicks, or Whitley's Veronica/speedwell.

Name/Origin/History: Pussytoes are native to the North American Prairies. The word *antennaria* in its botanical name refers to the plant's blooms that resemble insect antennae, while *rosea* means "pink."

Pros: Pussytoes require no maintenance, and the plant doesn't need any attention in the summer, either.

Cons: It doesn't tolerate waterlogged soil very well.

Tips: Cut off dead flowers on the pussytoes plant right to the leaves for a tidier look.

Rose Campion
Lychnis coronaria

People who love bright colours will fall in love with this perennial. Pictures don't do justice to the brilliant magenta rose campion offers to the landscape. If this colour is too much, however, a white version also exists. The small, eye-catching blossoms appear in midsummer above the silver-hued foliage. While often deemed a perennial, rose campion is so short-lived in the garden that it should be treated as a biennial. The silvery fuzzy leaves of the rose campion reflect the plant's ability to thrive in periods of high summer heat, making it a fine choice for prairie growing. This plant is quite drought-tolerant, though it does benefit from spot-watering during hot weather. If you want more plants, allow this vibrant bloomer to reseed, and resist the desire to deadhead for the last few flowers of the season. This is one perennial that doesn't need to be planted in abundance to make a splash; planting more than a small number may overpower other bloomers. It was my father-in-law who first introduced me to this pretty perennial, native to his home country in the Balkans, and I thank him for it.

QUICK NOTES

Perennial Type: Clumping border plant.

Top Choice Varieties: 'Alba' (white), 'Angel's Blush' (white with magenta eye).

Flower Colour and Type: Single saucer-shaped flowers in magenta or white.

Foliage Colour and Texture: Silver oval-shaped leaves with a fuzzy texture.

Size: Large—60-90 cm tall and 30-40 cm across.

Site Location: Plant rose campion in full sun to part shade in well-drained soil.

Perfect Partners: Behind cushion spurge; with lamb's ear for a silver effect.

Name/Origin/History: Native to the former Yugoslavia, Greece, and Turkey, the word *lychnis* is Greek for "lamp," while *coronaria* refers to a crown or garland. The common name "rose campion" has been used since the Renaissance and may mean "champion," as the flowers were used in garlands given to athletic victors.

Pros: The rose campion is an interesting hardy plant that isn't prone to pests or disease.

Cons: It's very short-lived, and its colour can be overpowering to other flowers.

Tips: Leave some dead flowers in place on the plant to allow it to reseed.

*In ancient Europe, the fuzzy leaves of the rose
campion plant were commonly used as lamp wicks.*

Rudbeckia adds a blast of colour to late-season gardens. There are twenty-five species of rudbeckia, all native to North America.

Rudbeckia

Rudbeckia fulgida var. *sullivantii*

A cousin of the coneflower, rudbeckia, or black-eyed Susan as it is often referred to, is another prairie native that should be in everyone's garden. Its deep yellow blooms arrive in early August, when many other perennials are finished their show, and they continue right up until the first hard frost. Rudbeckia really stands out in the garden, and the deep yellow petals contrast beautifully with the flower's chocolate-brown centres. These plants prefer evenly moist organic soil (add compost regularly), and do well with biweekly (in the heat) to weekly spot-watering during the summer. Like the coneflower, rudbeckia may fall victim to powdery mildew, so make sure it's in an open area where the breeze can touch it. It's also important to thin out rudbeckia plants in the spring, to prevent mildew and keep them looking lush. For daisy-lovers, rudbeckia is a must. The blooms are big and bold, so in a small area, one rudbeckia cultivated for accent may be sufficient, so as not to overpower other plants in your garden. Though a late summer bloomer, the bright yellow colour is well worth the wait. Rudbeckia is one perennial that will make people attending your late summer barbecues stand up and take notice of your garden.

QUICK NOTES

Perennial Type: Herbaceous clump-forming border.

Top Choice Varieties: 'Goldsturm' (yellow with dark brown centre).

Flower Colour and Type: Big yellow daisy-like flowers with chocolate-brown centres.

Foliage Colour and Texture: Large deeply jagged leaves, heavily veined with dark green colour. The plant has a bushy appearance.

Size: Large—45-60 cm tall and 30-45 cm across.

Site Location: This plant likes full sun but will tolerate some afternoon shade. Place rudbeckia plants near the back of a border.

Perfect Partners: Beside coneflower, globe thistle, blazing star, or sage.

Name/Origin/History: The rudbeckia plant was named after the seventeenth-century Swedish botanist Olaus Rudbeck (1630-1702), and is native to North America. The Latin word *fulgida* translates to "shining" or "glistening," referring to the flower petals. The word *sullivantii* refers to American botanist and plant documenter William Starling Sullivant (1803-1873).

Pros: The rudbeckia plant produces big, beautiful blooms.

Cons: It may become infected with powdery mildew and is prone to aphid attacks.

Tips: The name "rudbeckia" applies to several annuals and nonhardy perennials, as well as hardy perennials. Make sure you look at the plant tag carefully to ensure you have the plant you seek.

Sage
Salvia x *sylvestris*

The word "sage" is often generically used in gardening circles—I've heard it used to refer to anything from artemisia to rose campion, though not always correctly. The reason is that there are over nine hundred species of perennial, annual, and biennial sage worldwide. For our purposes, "sage" is the common name of *Salvia* x *sylvestris*, a spiked perennial hybrid with tons of appeal. If you love indigo, this is your plant, though white and pink types are also available. A member of the mint family, sage is an easy-to-care-for perennial with tube-like summer-blooming flowers and an upright trim look. It's superb in the landscape as a feature plant or planted in groups of three. Sage blooms for up to two months if spent flowers are removed. Like the culinary herb used in turkey seasoning, perennial sage has a strong aroma that people either like or detest. Sage can be divided if more plants are required. Sometimes perennial sage is sold under the label *Salvia* x *superba*, though there is little distinction between the two types. Sage likes the heat and doesn't require much watering, meaning it will look just as good when you return from summer vacation as when you left.

QUICK NOTES

Perennial Type: Herbaceous clump-forming border or edger.

Top Choice Varieties: 'May Night' (indigo), 'Rose Queen' (pink).

Flower Colour and Type: Small tubular blooms on erect stalks in indigo, violet, pink, and white.

Foliage Colour and Texture: Rough bright green leaves that are heart-shaped at the base and slimmer (lance-shaped) further up the stems.

Size: Medium to large—30-75 cm tall and 30-60 cm across.

Site Location: Plant sage in full sun. It can be grown in either organic or poor soil. It tolerates drought very well, and doesn't need much water once it's established.

Perfect Partners: With blue fescue grass and sedum varieties.

Name/Origin/History: While sage plants originate from throughout the globe, *sylvestris* is a hybrid of *s. nemorosa*, a native of Europe and central Asia. The word *salvia* in Latin means "to heal," while *sylvestris* translates to "of the woods" or "growing wild." The word "sage" probably comes from the Old French word *sauge* meaning "save," possibly referring to the healing properties of the plant.

Pros: Sage is a neat and tidy perennial that's super easy to grow and has a long blooming time.

Cons: The scent of the sage plant can be overpowering for some, and powdery mildew can be a nuisance.

Tips: The aromatic leaves of the sage plant are said to deter cats, so if felines are a nuisance in your neighbourhood, try planting strong-scented varieties like 'May Night.'

The healing properties of sage ('May Night' pictured here) go back to ancient times. It was first recorded in the writings of the Roman statesman Pliny.

In their natural alpine habitats, saxifrages can be found growing between rocks, which gives them a busted-through appearance.

Saxifrage, Encrusted/Rockfoil
Saxifraga paniculata

For some reason, many people are surprised that low-growing alpine plants do well on the Prairies. My friend Drew scrambles and climbs mountains on the weekends and was dumbfounded when I suggested he grow alpine plants like encrusted saxifrage in his backyard. While Drew seemed intrigued by growing plants like the ones adorning the mountains he regularly trekked, he'd never given any thought to including them in his landscape. Encrusted saxifrage is the perfect plant for those who love alpine plants but are worried about any special growing requirements that may exist. This plant is a low-grower, forming rosettes that kind of resemble hens and chicks. Each rosette is encrusted or edged with a white lime deposit, adding to the plant's interest. In midsummer, a 15-cm shoot rises up from the plant, and tiny star-shaped blooms emerge. After flowering, the single plant dies (similar to hens and chicks) but quickly becomes surrounded by more individual plants. Encrusted saxifrages don't tolerate hot sites well and benefit from a location that's sheltered from the blazing rays of the afternoon sun. Excellent in rock gardens and at the front of a partly shaded border, this ground cover adds interest, texture, and is tough. Sure to appeal to mountain climbers and couch potatoes alike, encrusted saxifrage "rocks"!

QUICK NOTES

Perennial Type: Evergreen rosettes that form a mat.

Flower Colour and Type: Tiny white star-shaped blooms.

Foliage Colour and Texture: Grey-green rosettes with spoon-shaped leaves; some appear to be rimmed with a white lime coating.

Size: Small—5-10 cm tall and 20-40 cm across. Bloom stalks rise up to 30 cm above the plant.

Site Location: Plant encrusted saxifrage in part sun to part shade, making sure the plants are shaded from the afternoon sun. These plants dislike moist areas. Check tags for specific growing conditions.

Perfect Partners: In front of fernleaf bleeding heart, or in a partly shaded rock garden near pinks.

Name/Origin/History: The encrusted saxifrage plant is native to the mountainous regions of the northern hemisphere. The word *saxifraga* means "rock breaker" in Latin. The Latin *paniculata* means "clusters of flowers on separate stalks."

Pros: This is an easy, unique plant that doesn't need much room to look great.

Cons: The encrusted saxifrage can be picky about its location. Make sure to avoid overly sunny spots and ensure there is adequate shade.

Tips: To avoid winter dieback, make sure that plants are mulched well during the winter.

Snow in Summer
Cerastium tomentosum

If you're looking for a plant that actually thrives on neglect, this is it! Snow in summer is a mat-forming ground cover that will quickly fill in a hot, dry space, without taking over the garden with military-like zeal. One small plant in the spring will develop into a 30-cm mat by late summer. Snow in summer looks great as an accent plant, as the silvery foliage adds interest to a leafy green border. The flowers of this tough little plant are pure white and glow brightly during summer evenings. Blooms appear in abundance in late spring, and then sporadically continue until early fall. I'm not sure why, but many experienced gardeners look down their noses at this drought-loving perennial. Maybe this is because snow in summer is extremely easy to grow and makes even the most inept gardener look like a seasoned pro. Though deemed invasive by some, snow in summer responds well to being mowed or severely cut back if it covers too much area. Snow in summer is one sun worshipper that won't go unnoticed.

QUICK NOTES

Perennial Type: Herbaceous mat-forming ground cover.

Top Choice Varieties: 'Yo-yo' (bright white flowers on a compact plant).

Flower Colour and Type: Small white flowers with lemon-coloured eyes.

Foliage Colour and Texture: Woolly silver-coloured foliage; leaves are small and spear-like.

Size: Small to medium—15-30 cm tall and 45-60 cm across.

Site Location: This plant likes full sun, in a dry, well-drained location. It looks great as a feature plant.

Perfect Partners: With 'Dragon's Blood' sedum and pink-flowering thyme.

Name/Origin/History: Snow in summer is a native of Sicily, Italy. The word *cerastium* in its botanical name is derived from the Greek *keros* ("horn"), which refers to the shape of the plant's seed covering. The word *tomentosum* ("fuzzy") makes reference to the hairs on the leaves and stems.

Pros: Snow in summer is very easy to grow.

Cons: It may spread too quickly for some gardeners.

Tips: Cut the plant back in midsummer after the initial burst of blooms has faded.

A true drought-lover, snow in summer needs very little water once it's established. Snow in summer has existed in prairie gardens since the early 1900s.

Soapwort is commonly called "Bouncing Bets," which comes from a nickname once given to English barmaids ("Betsies" or "Bets") during the Industrial Revolution. They used soap made from the plant's roots to clean beer bottles.

Soapwort, Rock
Saponaria, ocymoides

My friend and fellow hardcore gardener Diana first introduced me to rock soapwort. Diana is very choosy about what goes into her gardening space, and only tough, non-invasive plants make the cut. Diana lives on an acreage in southern Alberta's Chinook zone, where the climate is volatile, to say the least. This makes perennial survival a challenge. Second, two large Labrador retrievers bounce around her yard at will, often knocking down and excavating anything in their paths. If a plant thrives in Diana's yard, like rock soapwort does, without getting dug up or dying from exposure, it's a definite must-have. It's a superb ground cover that explodes with tiny star-shaped blooms in late spring and then sporadically throughout the summer. While it has a short lifespan (three to four years at most), rock soapwort is a prolific self-seeder. Allowing the plant to go to seed will ensure that it has a continued spot in the garden. Midsummer soapwort benefits from being clipped back, which may encourage a flush of blooms in the fall. If an easy-care, bright-blooming ground cover that tolerates dog abuse sounds like your kind of plant, add rock soapwort to your gardening scheme.

QUICK NOTES

Perennial Type: Herbaceous mat-forming ground cover.

Top Choice Varieties: 'Rubra Compacta' (small leaves with red flowers).

Flower Colour and Type: Tiny star-shaped flowers in light pink, purple, red, and white.

Foliage Colour and Texture: Small oval leaves with a rich green colour.

Size: Small—10-15 cm tall and 20-45 cm across.

Site Location: Plant rock soapwort in full sun at the front of a border, rock garden, or trailing over the edge of a raised bed.

Perfect Partners: Beside sedum, or in front of day lily.

Name/Origin/History: Native to the European Alps and the Pyrenees, both the botanical and common names of this plant refer to its association with soap, which was once commonly derived from its leaves and roots. The species name *ocymoides* means "basil-like" and refers to the shape of the plant's leaves.

Pros: This is an easy-care perennial that isn't bothered by bugs or disease.

Cons: Rock soapwort is short-lived in the garden (three to four years).

Tips: Allowing some flowers on the plant to develop seeds will result in more plants the following spring. Cut it back in midsummer and reblooming might occur in the fall.

Spurge, Cushion
Euphorbia polychroma

There's no perennial that shows off neon yellow and green quite like the cushion spurge. This plant has colourful, tropical-looking leaves and a neat and tidy appearance. It's also one of the most drought-tolerant plants in my yard. Being a sucker for bright colour, when I first saw pictures of the cushion spurge, I thought surely photo enhancement was involved in producing such a vibrant plant. After the plant first bloomed for me, I realized I was wrong; cushion spurge is really that radiant—it doesn't need photo touch-ups to sparkle. An interesting note about cushion spurge is that it doesn't flower, well, not in the traditional sense. It produces bright yellow bracts that open in May or June. A bract is a modified and often brightly coloured leaf, with a flower in its axil. Though a wonderful-looking perennial, cushion spurge is quite toxic and may irritate any skin that brushes up against it. This plant is so "hot" that its latex (a milky sap-like substance found in the leaves and stems) is said to burn away warts, but I wouldn't try this at home. Preferring hot, dry areas and not picky about what kind of soil it's in, cushion spurge is a plant that makes you look like a great gardener, even though it's really quite easy to take care of.

QUICK NOTES

Perennial Type: Clumping shrub-like perennial.

Flower Colour and Type: Nearly neon yellow bracts with small flower clusters in the middle.

Foliage Colour and Texture: Bright green or purple leaves and stems.

Size: Medium—40 cm tall and 40-60 cm across.

Site Location: Plant cushion spurge in full to part sun in hot, dry locations or mixed borders. This plant tolerates either poor or regular soil conditions.

Perfect Partners: Beside blue fescue grass, or in front of rose campion.

Name/Origin/History: Native to Germany, the Ukraine, and Greece, the cushion spurge is named after the ancient Greek physician Euphorbus (see picture caption). The plant's species name, *polychroma*, refers to its two-toned colouring. The word "spurge" comes from the Latin *expurgare* or "to cleanse," as the milky latex of the plant was once used as a laxative.

Pros: This is a drought-resistant plant with a tidy appearance and brilliant yellow spring colour. It tends to be pest- and disease-free.

Cons: The cushion spurge is toxic and may experience winterkill.

Tips: Make sure this plant is well mulched over the winter to give it added protection.

According to Roman historian Pliny (23-79 CE), it's believed King Juba II of Mauritania (52 BCE-27 CE) discovered Euphorbia polychroma, *or cushion spurge, in the first century BCE. It's named after Euphorbus, Juba's Greek physician, who found medicinal purposes for the plant's latex.*

Stonecrop ('Dragon's Blood' pictured here) is the perfect Saturday gardening choice, requiring no additional watering other than rainfall during the summer. This has made it a popular choice for the green roof movement in Germany and Scandinavia.

Stonecrop
Sedum spp.

Stonecrop is the perfect plant for people with kids; when a portion of it is broken off, it can be stuck in the ground to reroot, no questions asked. This is actually a regular occurrence in my backyard and, needless to say, I grow several types of stonecrop. These perennials are quite varied and many love the prairie climate. Commonly known by its botanical name, sedum, stonecrop is available in an array of shapes and sizes, including upright types, mounding domes, and creeping ground covers. Grown for both their succulent foliage and brightly coloured blooms, there is literally a sedum for everyone. Flowering of the plant depends upon the species and may occur anytime between spring and fall. Stonecrop plants do extremely well in hot, dry areas where the soil is poor; the only conditions they dislike are shaded areas with lots of moisture. Stonecrop looks great at the edge of a hot, dry border, trailing over raised beds, or even planted in containers (not upright containers, though). For people who hate watering, stonecrop is the ideal plant, as it looks best when you leave it alone.

QUICK NOTES

Perennial Type: Evergreen or semi-evergreen succulents available as edgers and ground covers.

Top Choice Varieties: Upright—'Neon' (bright pink blooms in fall), 'Autumn Joy' (mauve blooms in fall); mounding—Russian stonecrop (green or variegated leaves and orange flowers in summer); creeping—'Dragon's Blood' (red blooms in summer), 'Bronze Carpet' (pink blooms in summer).

Flower Colour and Type: Clusters of bright red, pink, yellow, and orange flowers; tall varieties flower in dome-shaped clusters, while ground cover varieties are often star-shaped.

Foliage Colour and Texture: Fleshy thick leaves that form ovals or rosettes in green, blue, red, bronze, or variegated patterns.

Size: Upright—medium to large—40-60 cm tall and 30-40 cm across; mounding—medium to small—20-25 cm tall and 30-35 cm across; creeping—small—10-15 cm tall and 40-60+ cm across.

Site Location: Plant stonecrop in hot, dry locations, in raised beds or, if creeping, in containers.

Perfect Partners: With snow in summer (red-foliage-type stonecrop), and with blue fescue ornamental grass (pink-flowering stonecrop).

Name/Origin/History: There are over three hundred species of sedum native to temperate regions throughout the globe. The word *sedum* comes from the Latin *sedere* or "to sit," referring to the way in which some species seem to emerge from rocks in an almost splattered kind of way. The common name, "stonecrop," comes from this reference.

Pros: Stonecrops need very little attention to look great and attract few pests.

Cons: Too much water can kill them quickly.

Tips: Broken stems from the plant can simply be placed back into the ground and will reroot with no questions asked.

Thrift
Armeria maritima

Pink lollipops sticking out of a clump of grass present a clear visual of thrift. Offering appeal on several levels, thrift is a small perennial that should exist in every prairie garden. Here's why: first, it's highly adaptable to prairie life, meaning it survives cold winter and summer drought without a lot of extra help. Second, its grassy leaves look cool from spring to fall. Third, and most important, it doesn't take up a lot of space, yet it adds punch to the landscape with its vibrant pink-candy-like blooms that last from June to September. Thrift is a plant that prefers cooler temperatures and low humidity, making it an ideal choice for the prairie garden. It's also extremely tolerant of salt, so if you plant it near the curb, you needn't worry about what winter road crews might dump on it. Planted individually, a clump of thrift at the front of the garden makes a good conversation piece. If you want a sea of pink, try grouping three plants together and soon a cushion of lollipops will form. Great in a backyard overrun by children, thrift won't mind an occasional posy-picking.

QUICK NOTES

Perennial Type: Evergreen mat-forming ground cover.

Top Choice Varieties: 'Dusseldorf Pride' (vibrant pink blooms).

Flower Colour and Type: Lollipop-like blooms in shades of bright pink and white.

Foliage Colour and Texture: Grass-like glossy deep green leaves.

Size: Small—15-20 cm tall and 30 cm across.

Site Location: Plant thrift near the front of a border or rock garden in full sun. This plant tolerates poor soil, and no special growing requirement, other than good drainage, is needed.

Perfect Partners: Near artemisia, stonecrop, or soapwort.

Name/Origin/History: Thrift is native throughout the coastal regions of Europe. The word *armeria* is derived from the Latin word for "carnation," while *maritima* refers to the sea. The name "thrift" probably comes from the plant's ability to thrive in poor soil situations.

Pros: Thrift has few enemies in the garden.

Cons: It can die out quickly in the middle of the plant.

Tips: If thrift plants look drab, cut them back close to the ground to rejuvenate them.

*There's a saying in Britain that people who grow
thrift in their gardens will never be poor.*

In ancient Europe, thyme ('Elfin' pictured here) was commonly burned as incense and placed in coffins to ensure safe passage to the afterlife. In Egypt, it was also used in the embalming process.

Thyme, Woolly
Thymus pseudolanuginosus

Though tiny in stature, these perennials offer a lot to the landscape. Woolly thyme has a fuzzy appearance and is extremely low to the ground. Another popular variety, creeping thyme (*Thymus serpyllum*), is hairless. Both are commonly planted between paving stones, hanging over the edge of raised beds, or at the front of a perennial border. Thyme is delicate in appearance but can tolerate a reasonable amount of foot traffic. Once the tiny blooms (arriving in midsummer) and leaves are walked on and bruised, they release that pleasant thyme scent that fills the air. These tiny wonders are amazingly drought-tolerant, and like most plants that love dry conditions, well-drained soil is a must. It's important, however, that woolly thyme gets enough winter protection. I've actually lost young plants by uncovering them too early in the growing season. Used for its ornamental properties over its culinary use, woolly thyme will quickly become a favourite in your garden. Used extensively since ancient times and mentioned in the writings of Shakespeare's *A Midsummer Night's Dream* (2.1), this perennial has long been associated with fairies. Thyme, with its elfin leaves, will add that special bit of romanticism to your garden paths.

QUICK NOTES

Perennial Type: Evergreen mat-forming ground cover.

Flower Colour and Type: Tiny pink or purple flowers.

Foliage Colour and Texture: Tiny fuzzy dark green round leaves.

Size: Small—1-3 cm tall and 30-45 cm across.

Site Location: Plant woolly thyme in full sun, in a dry, well-drained location. This plant does well between paving stones or cascading over the edge of a raised bed.

Perfect Partners: Beside hens and chicks or 'Dragon's Blood' sedum.

Name/Origin/History: Thyme is native to Europe, Asia, and North Africa. The word *thymus* in its botanical name comes from a Greek word meaning "to burn or sacrifice," referring to the plant's use in ancient rituals. The word *pseudolanuginosus* translates to "false wool," referring to the plant's fuzzy leaves.

Pros: Woolly thyme is easy to care for and tolerates being stepped on.

Cons: If the plant becomes waterlogged, winter dieback may occur.

Tips: Plant woolly thyme close to walkways where its aroma can be enjoyed.

Veronica/Speedwell, Whitley's
Veronica whitleyii

How I love this little plant! While the taller types of Veronica/speedwell are commonly grown in prairie gardens, Whitley's variety is not, though it should be. While I have regularly found it at big-box stores, I have not seen this low-grower in many gardens. In the spring, this tough ground cover bursts with tiny blue blooms dotted with white centres. Whitley's is another sun-loving ground-hugger that doesn't mind poor soil and droughty conditions. Though tough, it has a fine, delicate texture, making it a great choice for rock gardens, between paving stones, or in containers. A bonus of this diminutive plant is that it's easily pulled apart and replanted if more are required. It will quickly fill in an area, without becoming a nuisance. Whitley's also works to cover up the dying foliage of spring bulbs like tulips. If you prefer spiky types, woolly speedwell (*Veronica incana*) is an equally hardy option with similar growing requirements. With drought-loving plants becoming the rage with ecologically sensitive gardeners, Whitley's Veronica/speedwell is sure to grow in popularity.

QUICK NOTES

Perennial Type: Evergreen ground cover.

Flower Colour and Type: Tiny blue flowers, often with white centres.

Foliage Colour and Texture: Small fuzzy grey-green leaves.

Size: Small—5-10 cm tall and 30-60 cm across—it grows fast.

Site Location: Plant Whitley's Veronica/speedwell in full sun in poor to average soil that easily drains. This plant does well in containers or beside paving stones.

Perfect Partners: Near pussytoes (they bloom at the same time).

Name/Origin/History: Veronica species of plants are native throughout Europe and Asia, though it's unclear where Whitley's Veronica/speedwell comes from, or just who he or she was. The name "Veronica" is associated with Saint Veronica, who is said to have wiped Jesus' forehead as he carried the cross to Calvary. The word "speedwell" has its origins in the archaic European use of the word "speed," which once meant "to thrive."

Pros: Whitley's Veronica/speedwell will quickly fill in an area and doesn't require much care or attention.

Cons: This plant may be hard to find when shopping later in the growing season.

Tips: Cut back Whitley's after its blooming period in the spring and you might get a second flowering in the fall.

*Whitley's Veronica/speedwell looks great in a raised bed or
container where its tiny blue flowers can be closely admired.*

Glossary

accent plant. A feature plant that is placed in the garden as a focal point (e.g., a single clump of "Karl Foerster" grass may be used as an accent to give height and texture to the garden).

allelopathic. Refers to the ability of some plants to release certain toxins that prevent certain other plants from germinating or thriving nearby.

amendment. Compost or manure added to the soil in order to improve texture and fertility.

annual. A plant that grows, blooms, sets seed, and then dies in one growing season.

bacteria. Soil micro-organisms that are responsible for many soil processes, including making nitrogen available. They are involved in breaking down organic material and sometimes causing disease.

bells. Hanging flowers that are hat-shaped (e.g., bellflower).

bract. A modified and often brightly coloured leaf, with a flower or inflorescence in its axil (e.g., poinsettia).

clumping. Plants that appear as a single entity in the garden. They form tight assemblages of leaves and flowers. Clumping perennials do not tend to be garden bullies.

crown. The part of the plant just above the ground from where the stem and roots descend.

cultivars. Cultivated varieties of a species distinguished by differences in colour, size, and foliage.

cups. Flowers that are bowl-shaped (e.g., poppy).

daisies. Flowers with a large disk centre and many ray-like petals (e.g., coneflower).

dappled sun. When rays of sunshine are partially blocked or broken up by objects such as fences, structures, and other plants.

deadhead. To remove the faded, dead, or declining blooms from a plant.

division. The method of rejuvenating drab perennials described further in Chapter 4.

drought-tolerant. Plants that exist for a prolonged period of time without receiving water.

ecosystem. The physical environment in which living things exist.

established. Refers to plants that have adjusted to being uprooted and replanted. This process usually takes two to three years.

evergreen. Perennials that, in part or full, retain live leaves throughout the winter.

eye. A coloured dot formed in a flower's centre.

feature plant. See accent plant.

flowerhead. The complete bloom of a plant including its petals and centre.

foliage. The leaves of a plant.

four-season interest. Describes plants that look good in the garden in spring, summer, fall, and winter.

full sun. Six or more hours of unblocked sunshine per day.

fungus. Organisms that are spread by spores, including mildew. Many plant diseases like powdery mildew are types of fungus.

globes. Blooms that are ball-shaped (e.g., thrift).

hardy. Tough enough to survive severe weather conditions.

herbaceous. Perennials that die to the ground every year after the fall frosts, only to re-emerge the following spring.

humus. Organic material in soil including dead leaves and animals.

invasive. Refers to plants, including weeds, that take over the garden in a harmful way.

landscape. A planned garden, including plants, structures, and ornaments.

larva. A juvenile insect.

latex. A milk-like fluid found in plants like poppies and cushion spurges.

mound-shaped. Perennials that create a tidy rounded appearance.

nomenclature. A set or system of names, especially used in science.

part shade. Less than four hours of dappled or unblocked sunshine per day.

part sun. Four to six hours of unblocked sunshine per day.

plumes. Feather-shaped flowers (e.g., astilbe).

rhizome. An underground stem that produces roots. It's one of the ways plants spread.

self-seed. Refers to plants that create and release seeds so new seedlings will emerge the next spring.

shade. Less than two hours of dappled or unblocked sunshine per day.

spikes. Flowers that appear on one elongated stalk (e.g., blazing star).

spot-watering. Watering only those plants that need it instead of soaking the whole garden.

sprays. Flowers that form on multiple stems and look like tree branches (e.g., creeping baby's breath).

stars. Five-petalled flowers (e.g., vinca).

thin out. Removing up to one-third of a plant's new shoots in the spring. This allows for proper airflow and is done to increase plant health and as a preventative measure against powdery mildew.

tubular flowers. Long, round, and hollow flowers. Hummingbirds adore them (e.g., honeysuckle vine).

umbels. Umbrella-shaped flowers (e.g., Maltese cross).

variegated. Leaves that are more than one colour, often white and green.

vigorous. Refers to plants that quickly fill in garden space. Be cautious, however, as some plants listed as "vigorous" may become garden bullies.

virus. An infection that spreads in plants and is often transmitted via insects.

well-drained soil. Refers to soil where water doesn't form lasting puddles but is easily absorbed.

winter interest. Plants left in place over the fall and winter that add texture and substance to the landscape.

winter protection. Using mulch, leaves, or evergreen boughs to cover plants in order to protect them from harsh weather.

Index

Dawn Vaessen has been a secondary social studies teacher for the past 10 years with the Calgary Catholic School District. She earned her BA. and B.Ed. from the University of Saskatchewan. In 2006, Dawn completed the Master Gardener training program at the Calgary Zoo under the tutelage of horticulturalist and radio personality, Jeff De Jong. Alongside Namaka Ridge Tree Farm, Dawn developed two successful gardening seminars in the Spring of 2007. Dawn lives in Calgary, though she still considers herself a farm kid from Landis, Saskatchewan.

PHOTO BY KELLY BECHARD

Notes